Changing China for Christ

Changing China for Christ

Lottie Moon

Nancy Drummond

CF4·K

10 9 8 7 6 5 4 3 2 1
Copyright © 2014 Nancy Drummond
Paperback ISBN: 978-1-78191-524-0
epub ISBN: 978-1-78191-534-9
mobi ISBN: 978-1-78191-537-0

Published by Christian Focus Publications,
Geanies House, Fearn, Tain, Ross-shire,
IV20 1TW, Scotland, U.K.
Tel: +44 (0)1862 871011
Fax: +44 (0)1862 871699
www.christianfocus.com
email: info@christianfocus.com

Cover design by Daniel van Straaten
Cover illustration by Jeff Anderson
Printed and bound in Denmark by Nørhaven

Contents

A Training College Trickster

A shiver of excitement coursed through Lottie as her bare feet touched the cool, smooth floorboards. She felt her way to the chair where her coat was waiting. Then she tugged the blankets off her bed, gathered them up, and slipped out into the pre-dawn darkness.

It was April Fool's Day, 1855, and fourteen-year-old Lottie crept across the dewy lawn toward the bell tower that controlled the every move of the girls enrolled at the Virginia Female Seminary. She slipped into the building and climbed the rickety wooden staircase. Adjusting her awkward armful of bedclothes, Lottie started up the ladder that led to the bell itself. At the top of the ladder, Lottie slid precariously onto the rafters, carefully balancing her load.

She reached out to the massive bell and grasped the clapper that hung from the center.

"Don't look down," she whispered into the moonlit tower. "Don't look down and you'll be fine."

Lottie wrapped her sheets and blankets around the clapper again and again until it was swaddled in a huge, soft mass of wool and cotton. Then she tied it all together with the belt from her coat. Mission accomplished!

She nimbly scrambled back along the rafters and down the ladder. She raced out of the tower and across the lawn. Catching her breath outside the dorm room door, Lottie slipped silently back into bed and lay grinning into the darkness. Eyes wide, she waited for the six o'clock wake up bell that she knew would not ring. As the darkness outside grayed to dawn and then full sunlight spilled into the room, Lottie's grin widened in triumph.

Just after seven o'clock, the bell finally rang. Lottie's roommate, Cary Ann, lifted her head and rubbed her eyes in confusion.

"Wasn't that the wake up bell? Why is it so light outside?" She glanced sleepily at Lottie, lying fully clothed on a bare mattress. Cary Ann sat up in surprise. "And what happened to all the blankets from your bed?"

Lottie just giggled.

Cary Ann shook her head, trying to suppress a smile. "Oh, Lottie," she said in mock exasperation, "what have you done this time?"

Charlotte Digges Moon—better known as Lottie Moon—was practically famous for her pranks and practical jokes, both at school and back home on the sprawling grounds of Viewmont, Lottie's childhood home. As a little girl, Lottie lived a carefree life among the 1500 rolling acres of one of the largest plantations in Albemarle County, Virginia. Nestled between the estates of two former presidents, and once a favorite retreat of the Governor of Virginia, Viewmont was a study in old southern luxury. But to Lottie, the rambling house and endless fields and orchards were the perpetual playground she called home.

For the first twelve years of her life, Lottie spent her days reading and running, wandering through her wide world with few rules and restrictions. Surrounded by six siblings and countless cousins, there was never a dull moment. Life was a whirlwind of carriage rides and crazy adventures, house guests and hide-and-seek. As for education, Lottie had all the knowledge she could desire in her father's extensive library, and she was largely left to educate herself. Faith was one of the few constants in the household, and adherence to biblical principles came above all other priorities.

Just weeks after her twelfth birthday, however, Lottie's life changed forever. Recently recovered from a life-threatening illness, Lottie's father headed for New Orleans and Memphis on business. As he traveled, the steamboat he was on caught fire, forcing the passengers to jump from the ship into the chilly January river water. Edward Moon jumped with the other passengers, dragging his heavy trunk of gold behind him. He managed to pull the trunk to shore and hoisted it onto his back, but it was more than his weakened body could handle. He collapsed on the shore and died.

When news of her father's death reached Viewmont a few days later, Lottie knew her world would never be the same. The house was wrapped in a blanket of grief—dark and uncertain. But as the days turned to weeks and then months, things began to come together again, and sunshine seeped back into Lottie's life. Edward Moon had always believed in the concept of higher education for all of his children, and he had left money in his will to make sure each of his children could pursue their dreams and attend any school they chose.

Formal education was a rarity for young ladies in the South at that time, and Lottie was ready for the adventure it would bring. So in the fall of 1854, a few months before her fourteenth birthday, Lottie joined nearly 100 other girls at the Virginia Female Seminary.

As she entered the large hall on her first day, Lottie felt very small. It was her first time away from home, and even though girlish chatter surrounded her, she felt very alone. But Lottie soon made friends and became known as a good student. She was especially bright in language studies, including English, French, and Latin. She also became editor of one of the school newspapers.

Students were allowed painfully little free time, a restriction that choked Lottie's carefree spirit. In rebellion, she developed a quick wit and a talent as a trickster, culminating in the April Fool's Day prank in the bell tower. Lottie's classmates loved her as a constant source of laughter and unexpected amusement, but her grades in behavior and deportment suffered as a result.

Despite her behavioral challenges and a bad habit of skipping required worship services during her last quarter of school, Lottie graduated on July 3rd, 1856. As she squirmed on the hard wooden bench and tugged impatiently at her itchy lace dress during the long graduation ceremony, Lottie looked at the eager faces of her classmates. Most of them would return to their fancy homes, eventually have fancy weddings, and begin fancy lives of their own. But Lottie wanted so much more than that!

She was nearly sixteen years old, full of life and energy, and armed with a good education. She felt like she was teetering on the edge of a promising future. All she lacked was direction. What should she do next?

Facing the Future

Without a sure sense of direction, all roads led Lottie back to Viewmont. With a sigh of relief, she settled back into her old pampered, carefree existence. She had servants to do her work and provide for her needs, leaving her free to indulge in parties and hayrides and concerts with her friends and cousins. It was fun, but Lottie felt a deep hollowness in her soul.

"Are you glad to be here with us, Lottie?" her littlest sister Edmonia asked one afternoon.

"Of course I am, Eddie," Lottie answered, ruffling the five-year-old's dark hair. "Can't you tell I am happy?"

"Well ... sometimes," Eddie admitted. "Most of the time, I guess. But other times you just seem so sad."

Mrs. Moon looked up from her sewing and studied Lottie's face. She understood Lottie's deep sadness, probably better than Lottie herself did. Mrs. Moon knew that Lottie had decided she wanted to have nothing to do with God or Jesus or religion or church. Mrs. Moon knew that Lottie's rejection of God was the main reason for her sadness and lack of direction, but she also knew that Lottie would have to understand that truth on her own time and in her own way.

"I have a plan," Lottie announced to her mother and Eddie a few days later. "I believe it is high time for Eddie to begin her education."

"Really?" Eddie asked, her face brightening. "But who will teach me?"

"I will, of course," Lottie insisted. "I didn't go to two years of training college to just sit here and do nothing."

Lottie plunged eagerly into teaching Eddie, planning lessons carefully and filling the days with poetry, plays, stories, and songs. Eddie was a quick learner, and the sisters spent many happy hours together studying and giggling. Lottie loved teaching Eddie, and she wondered if she had finally found her life path.

One autumn afternoon, Mrs. Moon rushed joyfully into the parlor where Lottie and Eddie were studying.

"Orie is coming home for Christmas," she declared, waving a letter vigorously. "She has finally finished her studies and she is coming home. Oh! It will be so good to see her!"

Lottie's older sister, Orianna—or Orie, as she preferred to be called—had been up north in Pennsylvania at medical school for several years. Upon graduation, Orie and one of her classmates had become the first two female doctors in the South. But even though Orie had all the necessary education, no one was willing to hire a female doctor in 1856. It just wasn't done. So Orie was headed home to visit Viewmont while she figured out what to do next.

Christmas arrived, and with it came Orie and hours of eye-opening conversation for Lottie. Like Lottie, Orie had abandoned the faith of her childhood in favor of intellectual reason.

"I don't have a problem with God," Orie told Lottie, "but I certainly don't need Him to bring meaning to my life. In fact, I don't need anyone to bring meaning to my life. I am the mistress of my own destiny."

Lottie nodded enthusiastically. "That's exactly how I feel! It's my life, and I want to live it my way."

Orie regaled Lottie with tales of the progressive thinking in the North. She was a devoted follower of Elizabeth Blackwell and Lucretia Mott, leaders of the women's rights movement.

"We call ourselves feminists," Orie declared with conviction. "We believe women can do anything men can do. And we believe we can do it as well as any man—maybe better!"

Lottie drank in these new ideas. She liked the idea that she could do anything she wanted to do. She embraced the concept of independence and empowerment. She couldn't wait to live her dreams... if only she could figure out what her dreams were.

As Lottie was looking for her future, she did not realize her future was actually taking shape not far away. The Virginia Baptists were forming a new type of school, founded by leading educators. The idea was to establish a college where women could earn a Bachelor's or Master's degree while studying the same subjects the men studied at the nearby University of Virginia. Higher education for women in the South was a brand new concept, and as soon as Lottie heard about it, she knew she wanted to be a part of it.

"Do you have to go away again?" Eddie asked as Lottie began packing her things. "I'm just getting good at learning new things."

Lottie sat on her flowered bedspread and pulled Eddie up beside her. "You are almost six-and-a-half now, Eddie," Lottie said solemnly. "I am trusting you to keep up your studies on your own. You are a good reader, and your French and other studies are growing stronger every day."

Eddie's eyes were wide. "Do you think I can do it, Lottie?"

"Well, of course you can!" Lottie smiled down at Eddie. "That is exactly how I learned when I was your age. And look at me now." She paused, then added, "You must write to me every week and tell me about your progress."

Eddie grinned. "I promise!"

In September 1857, Lottie said goodbye to her family and left to join the second class to enter the Albemarle Female Institute in Charlottesville, Virginia. She was determined to succeed, proving that women could accomplish anything they pleased. At almost seventeen, she was ready to take the world by storm.

As the rickety carriage rolled up the long drive to the school, however, Lottie's eyes grew wide. The

Albemarle Female Institute was an imposing, four-story brick building with real glass windows all along the front. A long staircase led to the two-story veranda flanked by four enormous stone pillars. Wide double doors led into an ornate front hall. Even Lottie was overcome with such grandeur.

After checking in, Lottie was shown to the boarding quarters nearby in a large building that had once been the Monticello Hotel.

"Lottie Moon!" a familiar voice called.

Lottie turned and spotted her old roommate from the Virginia Female Seminary. "Cary Ann Coleman!" she called back joyfully.

Cary Ann hurried over. "I'm so glad you're here," she confessed. "I was afraid I wouldn't know anyone. Shall we room together again?"

Lottie linked arms with Cary Ann. "Of course. We have to be roommates again. It will be just like old times!"

Cary Ann pulled back and studied Lottie carefully. "Just like old times?" she questioned. "With all the laughter and livelihood? And all the pranks?"

Lottie's eyes twinkled. "Were you expecting anything less?"

Cary Ann rolled her eyes and shook her head. "I guess not."

"Good," Lottie said. "Then let the adventure begin!"

Resistance is Futile

In no time at all, Lottie had reestablished herself as the most unpredictable and incorrigible member of her class. If there was a joke being told, Lottie was likely the teller. If there was a prank being played, Lottie was sure to be involved. If a witty remark was hurled at a professor, it probably came from Lottie's corner of the room.

After a particularly raucous day, one of Lottie's classmates approached her with an evil grin.

"Your name is Lottie D. Moon, right?"

Lottie nodded, a puzzled look on her face.

"Does the 'D' stand for 'Difficult'?" the classmate teased.

"Nope," Lottie shot back. "It stands for 'Devil'!"

Many of the girls came to believe that was true. Lottie was full of mischief, and she blatantly rejected any activity that had to do with God. She skipped worship services, tormented classmates during their devotions, and taunted those who spent time in prayer. On the first Sunday at Albemarle Female Institute, Cary Ann and the other girls put on their prettiest dresses and picked up their Bibles.

"Lottie, why aren't you dressed?" Cary Ann asked her roommate, who was lounging on her bed in an everyday dress.

"I am dressed," Lottie answered.

"You're wearing that to church?" a tall girl asked, her brows arching in disapproval.

"Don't be silly." Lottie dismissed them with a wave of her hand. "I have no intention of going to church."

Cary Ann's eyes pleaded silently with Lottie. "Reverend Broadus expects us at his services. And the church is just across the street. Don't you think…"

Lottie rolled her eyes at Cary Ann. "Are we required to go?"

"Well, not required exactly…" Cary Ann admitted hesitantly. "Be we are encouraged to attend."

"In that case …" Lottie said, bouncing up off her bed.

Cary Ann's face brightened as Lottie bounded across the room toward the bookshelf where her dusty Bible lay. But the smile disappeared when she snatched a copy of Shakespeare's *Twelfth Night* from the shelf.

"In that case," Lottie finished, "I will be in the field, leaning on a haystack, reading the day away."

"Oh, Lottie," Cary Ann moaned as the other girls hurried out the door. "There really is no hope for you."

All the other girls in the dorm left for church while Lottie left to find her haystack. It began a pattern that Lottie followed for her first year-and-a-half at the school. Remembering her conversations with Orie, Lottie was determined to be the "mistress of her own destiny," and she poked fun at anyone who submitted to a "higher power."

Despite the teasing and taunting, however, Lottie was never truly unkind, and she quickly became very popular among her classmates. She was smart and gifted, particularly in language subjects. By the end of her first year, Lottie had already earned a diploma in Latin, and she was at the top of her class in Greek, Italian, French, and Spanish. She was always willing to help her fellow students, and many relied on her for guidance.

In December 1858, halfway through Lottie's second year at Albemarle Female Institute, Reverend Broadus decided to hold some special church services every night and prayer meetings every morning. A few of the girls worked up the courage to invite Lottie to attend.

"We are having special revival services at church this week," a brave classmate said, sidling up to Lottie. "Would you like to attend with us?"

Lottie turned and smiled with the full brilliance of all her southern charm. "It's sweet of you to ask," she gushed, "but I've never seen a reason to go over to the church up to this point, and I don't see any real reason to start now."

The girl's shoulders slumped, and she and her friends walked away, shaking their heads. As Lottie watched them go, she felt a slight twinge in her stomach. For just a moment, she wondered if it were possible that all her friends were right about religion and God, and she was the one who was wrong. But it was a fleeting thought, and Lottie soon brushed her doubts away like wayward cobwebs. "I'm smart, intelligent and I know what I believe. Even if it does make my friends unhappy!"

Still, that night when the dormitory emptied just before the revival services, Lottie sat listlessly in her silent room. She couldn't help feeling a little lonely, and from her loneliness and boredom, a plan began to form. She suddenly knew exactly how to please her friends, stay true to herself, and gather valuable ammunition for future taunting—all at once!

The next night, Lottie put on her best dress and dusted off her Bible. She was waiting by the door when the other girls came downstairs.

"What are you doing?" Cary Ann asked.

"Going to the revival services with you, of course," Lottie replied. "Isn't that what you wanted?"

Cary Ann and the other girls eyed Lottie skeptically, but none of them dared challenge her. Lottie led their little procession across the street to the church, smirking all the way. She marched right to the front of the church and took a seat. Her classmates hesitantly filled in the pews beside her. They all knew Lottie was up to something, but they didn't know what.

Lottie smiled smugly as the service began. Her unspoken plan was to take mental notes on all the absurd things Reverend Broadus said. Then she would use the things she heard to taunt her faithful classmates later. She could hardly wait for the sermon to start—she was eager to spot all the illogical, ignorant ideas she just knew she was about to hear.

Halfway through the sermon, Lottie had a big problem. Everything Reverend Broadus said made sense. In fact, it was making her heart and mind buzz with confusion. Every Sunday School lesson she had heard as a child flooded back into Lottie's consciousness. Every story her mother had read out loud surged through her soul. Instead of gathering ammunition for her own private war on God, Lottie found herself nearing a point of surrender. What was happening to her?

Lottie was uncharacteristically quiet as she walked back to the dormitory and got ready for bed. The other girls didn't know what to think of this new pensive Lottie, so they kept quiet too. Lottie slipped into bed, hoping a sound sleep would clear away her uncertainties. But God had other plans.

As Lottie lay awake in the darkness, a dog began to bark down the street. Cary Ann was breathing deeply, lost in dreams, but the dog's incessant barking kept jolting Lottie awake. Truths from Reverend Broadus' sermon danced through her drowsy brain. Finally, Lottie knew what she had to do.

She climbed from beneath her cozy covers and knelt on the frigid floorboards. Shivering, she bowed her head and whispered into the night.

"God," she prayed, "it's been a long time since I've talked to You. But I guess I've always known You were there. I just wanted to live my own life in my own way."

Lottie heaved a deep sigh. "God, that strategy isn't really working for me anymore. I know I need You. So tonight, I give You my heart and life. Please forgive my sins and be the Lord of all I am. Teach me to follow You. Amen."

A peace Lottie could not explain washed over her body and soul, overpowering the cold December air and the emotions that had warred in her heart. She nestled back under her blankets, happier than she could remember feeling in a long, long time. As she drifted off to sleep, Lottie realized the dog in the distance had stopped barking. She smiled. Everything seemed to finally make sense, and she closed her eyes with a contented sigh.

Surprised murmurs rippled through the room as Lottie entered the morning prayer meeting the next day.

"What's she doing here?" a girl muttered.

"Probably came to poke fun and disrupt our services," another girl guessed.

"Two services in less than twenty-four hours?" observed a third classmate. "That's got to be some sort of record for Lottie!"

To their surprise, Lottie sat respectfully through the prayer meeting. She even participated. Everyone watching could tell something was different about Lottie Moon. She wasn't the same girl she had been the day before.

"Lottie, what happened to you?" Cary Ann asked as she walked back to the dormitory with Lottie. "It's obvious that something is very different about you."

Lottie stopped walking and grabbed Cary Ann's arm, her eyes sparkling with joy. "I gave my heart to Jesus!"

Cary Ann's eyes filled with tears. "Oh, Lottie! I'm so happy for you," she said. She paused, then added, "Do you know what we were doing in prayer meeting just before you walked in?"

Lottie shook her head.

"We were praying for you...praying that you would come and join us," Cary Ann told her.

"Really?"

"Really, Lottie! I am so happy you made this decision."

At the evening revival service that night, December 21, 1858, eighteen-year-old Lottie Moon walked to the front of the church and professed her faith in Jesus Christ. She was baptized the next night. Immediately, the other girls saw a change in Lottie's life. She was still funny and lively and bright, but there was a new gentleness and light that surrounded her spirit. The transformation was evident.

For her final two-and-a-half years at Albemarle Female Institute, Lottie led her classmates not only academically, but spiritually as well. She conducted prayer groups, organized Bible studies, taught Sunday school, attended multiple church services each week, and began to feel God truly directing her life. It was a time of great excitement and growth for Lottie.

After four years at school, Lottie graduated with a Master of Arts degree in the spring of 1861. She and four classmates became the first women in the South to earn Master's degrees. And because Lottie was at the top of her class in nearly every subject, Reverend Broadus declared her "the most educated woman in the South." It seemed twenty-year-old Lottie was ready to take on the world, but her world was about to turn completely upside down.

A World at War

On April 12, 1861, the Confederate Army from the South fired on Fort Sumter at Charleston Harbor in South Carolina. The Fort was manned by U.S. Army soldiers from the North, and the incident was the culmination of long months of complex disagreements between the northern and southern states. The artillery shots fired that day became the opening act in the Civil War.

By the time Lottie finished her courses and graduated, only a month later, the war was in full swing. Convictions ran high and blood ran hot when issues of slavery and states' rights—key points of contention— were raised. Lottie and her friends gladly proclaimed their loyalty to the South and southern ideals. They found the thought of war and fighting for one's beliefs to be romantic and exciting.

Energized by this atmosphere of conflict, Lottie returned to Viewmont after graduation. Wrapped securely in the comforts of home, Lottie felt the war was far away and irrelevant. She was much more excited about the fact that Orie was also home at Viewmont. Orie had traveled the world for the past few years, visiting famous cities like Paris and Cairo, looking for places to use her medical skills.

Orie finally found herself in Jerusalem with her Uncle James, who was a missionary there. James Barclay, Lottie's mother's older brother, was a doctor who had left a promising practice in the South to minister in Jerusalem. He was more than happy to let Orie help out around his clinic, which doubled as a mission. As Uncle James worked with Orie, he wove faith into every conversation. Soon Orie found herself convicted and convinced, just as Lottie had been. Orie accepted Jesus as her Savior, and Uncle James baptized her in a river outside Jerusalem.

Lottie and Orie found the bond of belief in God was stronger than the faith they had shared in feminism.

"But don't think I can't still take care of myself," Orie insisted as she sat on the veranda at Viewmont with Lottie and Eddie one early summer afternoon. "Following Jesus doesn't make me any less of a strong woman. Believe me—I've proven it!"

Lottie lifted her eyebrows and studied her big sister. "I sense a story behind that statement."

Orie grinned mischievously and glanced at Eddie. "Most certainly! But the story may be too much for our littlest sister," she teased.

"Oh, Orie—please tell me! Please?" Eddie begged. "Lottie, tell her. Tell her how grown up I am now!"

Lottie and Orie exchanged amused glances. "She is ten years old now," Lottie pointed out.

"Is she now? Well then, I suppose she is old enough to hear all about my adventure. It all began on a ship's deck in the middle of the Atlantic Ocean …"

Orie told how she had been in her cabin on a ship when she needed some fresh air. As she stood by herself near the railing on the upper deck, enjoying the salt-tinged breeze on her face, an unshaven sailor with an evil gleam in his eye stepped up alongside her.

"Aren't you nervous traveling alone?" he had asked, laying a menacing hand on her shoulder. "All sorts of things could happen to a pretty lady like you without an escort."

Orie said she shrugged his hand off her shoulder, reached under her dress, and pulled out a small pistol. Without even a second's hesitation, she aimed across the water and pulled the trigger. In the distance, a seagull dropped from the sky.

"Oh, I'm not worried," Orie had said. "Are you worried?"

Orie told Lottie and Eddie the sailor backed away as his evil expression melted into a face of fear.

"He didn't speak to me again for the rest of the journey," Orie said, laughing. "In fact, when he saw me coming, he headed the other way!"

Lottie grinned at her sister with newfound respect. She loved the way Orie could mix a surrendered life with a strong spirit. That was exactly what Lottie wanted to be—faithful while being fearless, and sweet-spirited while being strong. She had a gnawing desire to do something that would make a difference, something that really mattered.

Lottie soon had her chance to start making a difference, as July 1861 brought the Battle of Bull

Run, the first major, large-scale clash of the Civil War. It was a bloody, bitter conflict, and the war that had seemed romantic and exciting from afar was suddenly painful and ugly as it hit close to home. Even though the South had won the battle, so many men had been seriously wounded that the army was desperate for doctors. Orie immediately reported for duty, and even though she was a woman doctor, they gladly accepted her help. Lottie and two of her younger sisters—Colie and Mollie—went along as nurses.

They were unprepared for what they found. Dirty, injured men were everywhere in the makeshift hospitals, some crying out in pain and others writhing in silent agony. The scent of fear and death clung to the rafters, and hopelessness colored everything a dismal gray. Lottie wanted to help, but she was secretly thankful when she was sent home to Viewmont to handle hospital correspondence and administrative paperwork. With her brother Ike away fighting in the war and her sisters helping in the battlefield hospitals, Mrs. Moon desperately needed Lottie to help run Viewmont and supervise Eddie's education. Lottie felt more useful at sunny Viewmont than on the battlefield.

The war dragged on much longer than anyone expected. After a few months, Orie was exhausted and run down. She came home to Viewmont, and Lottie added nursing Orie back to health as one of her primary duties. The skills Lottie had learned during her short time in the battlefield hospital served her well, and Orie was feeling better in no time.

While Orie was healing, a young army doctor visited her. They had met in a battlefield hospital, and the doctor was concerned when Orie was sent home. He came to Viewmont to make sure she was well cared for and healing properly. Before long, they were in love and were married. When Orie was feeling better, she joined her husband, John, in the capital of the South at Richmond, Virginia. But before long, Orie became pregnant. She left John in Richmond, close to the battlefield action, and she returned to the relative safety of Viewmont. John visited whenever he could, and by the end of the war, he and Orie had three little boys.

In April 1865, word came that General Robert E. Lee from the South surrendered to General Ulysses S. Grant from the North. The Civil War was officially over, ending with an agreement at the Appomattox Courthouse, just forty miles south of Viewmont. With the war ended, the northern soldiers who had invaded the South were turned loose into the countryside. They looted and burned their way recklessly back to the North.

On a sunny late-spring afternoon, a servant stumbled into the yard at Viewmont, sweat beading on his brow, his breath coming in short, labored puffs.

"They's burning Carter's Mill," he panted. "Viewmont's sure to be next. You ladies best be gettin' out while you can."

The women sprang into action, loading all their most precious belongings into a wagon. In the downstairs parlor, Mrs. Moon grabbed Lottie's arm and thrust two heavy pillowcases into her hand.

"This is all the silver," Mrs. Moon said. "Some of it has been in the family for generations. Take it and bury it in the orchard. And hurry!"

Lottie grabbed the pillowcases and dashed haphazardly into the cool, shady orchard. She hastily buried the silver and ran back to the house to help her mother.

When all the valuables were loaded, a servant drove the wagon into the woods. The family waited for hours in tense silence, ready to defend their home. But the anticipated raids never came. Finally, a neighbor came by and told them the burning of Carter's Mill had been nothing more than a rumor. The bands of looters were miles away, and Viewmont was safe.

Someone was sent to bring the wagon of valuables home, and Lottie and Eddie went to the orchard to dig up the silver.

"Where did you bury it?" Eddie asked.

Lottie looked around in the gathering darkness. All the trees were suddenly identical.

"I think it was here," Lottie said uncertainly.

Lottie and Eddie dug vigorously, but found nothing.

"I guess you were wrong."

"It would seem so," Lottie agreed, wiping trickles of sweat from her brow. She looked around.

"Maybe it was over there...yes, I'm fairly certain it was."

They dug again, but again found nothing. After several more tries, Lottie began to feel desperate.

"It's getting dark, Lottie," Eddie pointed out. "What if we can't find it?"

"Then we will come back in the morning. And we will start looking all over again."

They never found the silver. In her haste and fear, Lottie had paid no attention to where she buried the family treasures. They were gone forever, and Lottie felt guilty and responsible. Little did she know, the lost silver was only the beginning of her family's struggles.

Post-War Practicality

Like many other southern families, the Moon family emerged from the Civil War with only a fraction of their pre-war wealth, glory, and prestige. To show their commitment to the cause, wealthy southern families had been encouraged to donate their gold, silver, money, and other valuables to the war efforts. They were promised repayment in full when the South achieved victory. But victory never came, and neither did the promised repayment.

Faced with financial disaster, Mrs. Moon rented out the farmlands of Viewmont to help pay her debts. She also gave 400 acres to her son Ike and his wife for farming. Orie and John moved to Alabama to help his family. What little money remained was used to send Eddie and Mollie—the two youngest girls—to school. The family was fragmenting, and it meant new roles for everyone.

With her schooling complete and no husband to provide for her, Lottie was left with only one option: find a job. But this was not a frightening or negative thought to Lottie. Instead, she saw it as an exciting new adventure. She quickly spread the word among her friends and extended family that she was looking for a job, preferably a teaching position. It wasn't long before opportunities began to come in.

"Look at this one," Lottie said to her mother as they sat by the fire one spring evening. "Reverend Broadus wrote me about the Danville Female Academy in Kentucky. He says the principal, Reverend Selph, is looking for an efficient teacher and strong disciplinarian."

Mrs. Moon chuckled. "You didn't have much discipline when you were in school, but it certainly sounds perfect for you now."

Lottie smiled. "True. In fact, Reverend Broadus has recommended me for the position. And I've heard things in Kentucky are better than they are over here in Virginia." Lottie folded the letter from her old professor and mentor. "I believe I will write to Reverend Selph and make a formal application."

By summer, Lottie had been hired as a teacher in the preparatory department of the Danville Female Academy. She packed her belongings, said goodbye to her family, and headed to Danville, Kentucky. It was a new chapter in Lottie's life, and her first real chance at independence and making a life for herself.

The first year was difficult. Lottie was homesick and exhausted by adjusting to the duties of being a teacher. But she was determined, and by her second year of teaching, she had earned the respect and admiration of both her students and colleagues. Lottie was active in the local Baptist church, teaching Sunday School and even serving as the pastor's assistant, and she was always willing to lend a hand to those in need.

In the late spring of 1870, just as Lottie's fourth year at Danville was coming to a close, she received urgent news from Viewmont. Her mother was sick and not expected to live much longer. Lottie packed a few belongings and hurried home.

"I'm home, Mama," Lottie whispered as she knelt beside Mrs. Moon's bedside. "I'm here now."

Mrs. Moon's eyes fluttered open and she smiled weakly, raising a trembling hand to stroke Lottie's cheek. "My sweet Lottie. I knew you would come. There is so much to say and so little time."

Over the next several days, Lottie rarely left her mother's side. They talked of happiness and heartbreak. They talked about each of Lottie's siblings and the lives they had built for themselves. They talked about favorite memories of the past and hopes for the future. It was a time Lottie would always cherish.

On a sunny morning in late June, Mrs. Moon called those dearest to her into her bedroom. She told them how much she loved them and reminded them how much God loved them. Then she died peacefully, surrounded by family and friends.

After her mother's death, Lottie felt empty and lost. She spent the long summer days roving Viewmont, just as she had when she was a child. At nearly thirty years old, she felt like a small child again, wondering what the future would hold. To help fill the days, she and

Eddie often took buggy rides on the bumpy, dusty roads of Albemarle County. On one of those lazy afternoon rides, Eddie confided in Lottie.

"I think I know what I'm supposed to do with my life."

Lottie looked at her youngest sister in surprise. "What are you supposed to do?"

"I'm supposed to be a missionary to China."

Lottie smiled. "I've had that same thought myself— so many times! Ever since Mama read us the story of Ann Judson when I was just a little girl, I have dreamed of missionary work." Lottie turned to study Eddie carefully. "But foreign mission work would mean finding a husband. Did you have someone in mind?"

Eddie shook her head emphatically. "I intend to petition the Foreign Missions Board to let me go as a single woman, working with a missionary couple."

"They'll never let you go," Lottie warned, shaking her head and turning her attention back to the road. "They tried it once before, and it failed. They will never believe a single woman is capable of missionary work."

Eddie squeezed Lottie's arm gently. "Then we must make them believe."

At the end of the summer, Lottie returned to Danville to take a higher position as Chairperson of History, Grammar, Rhetoric, and Literature. But she couldn't get the conversation with Eddie out of her head. She felt like she needed to be reaching out more, doing more self-sacrifice. If she couldn't be a foreign missionary, perhaps she could be a missionary right where she was: in the war-ravaged South.

"Anna, do you think we are too comfortable here at Danville?" Lottie asked her best friend and colleague, Anna Safford, one afternoon.

"What do you mean by 'too comfortable'?"

"Well, we have good jobs and a steady paycheck. We work in a well-established school with well-educated colleagues and well-behaved students. We have all the resources we could ever need right here at our fingertips." Lottie waved her arms wide. "It isn't that I don't enjoy it. But sometimes I feel like it isn't much of a ministry."

Anna looked up in surprise. "I've been feeling the exact same way I feel like there's something more I should be doing."

"So what can we do?" Lottie wondered.

The friends soon had their answer. Lottie's cousin, Pleasant, was starting a school in Cartersville, Georgia. It was to be a private girls' school, and Pleasant needed two educated, capable women to get things up and running. Lottie and Anna jumped at the chance to work in a new school in the Deep South. As soon as the 1870-71 school year was complete at Danville, they boarded a train for Georgia.

The train ride to Cartersville was both eye-opening and heartbreaking. As they traveled deeper and deeper into the South, Lottie and Anna saw huddled bands of homeless people camping in tattered tents beside the tracks. Dirty, shoeless children played in the dust and watched the train pass with hollow, hopeless eyes. Battered by brutal battles, once-majestic buildings stood in crumbling silence. Estates along the route were abandoned and overgrown, and squatters peered from the windows as they passed. Lottie felt excitement build within her soul. Here was a mission field she could reach!

When Lottie and Anna finally reached Cartersville, they were astounded to find the schoolhouse was nothing more than an old three-room cannery with cracked and broken windows and a carpet of weeds and dust. Pleasant was apologetic as the two ladies looked over their new domain. But Lottie and Anna just exchanged amused grins.

"Don't apologize, Cousin," Lottie said. "We both love a challenge. That's what brought us here in the first place!"

After a few weeks of back-breaking work and mind-numbing planning, Lottie and Anna were ready to open the doors of the Cartersville Female High School. Classes began on July 3, 1871 with seven students, but within a few months, the school had grown to over 100 pupils! Lottie and Anna worked from dawn until dusk, pouring both extensive energy and financial resources into the new school.

Lottie had never been happier or more fulfilled. She felt like she was finally doing something that mattered, something that made a difference for God's Kingdom.

But the spring of her first year in Cartersville brought shocking news that unsettled Lottie and reawakened old doubts and desires.

The Makings of a Missionary

Lottie's hands trembled slightly as she read Anna the hastily scrawled letter she had just received.

"It has finally happened, Lottie," Eddie wrote in the letter. "I have been approved to go to China as a single female missionary! I will be living in Tengchow with the Crawford family. Isn't it exciting?"

Lottie folded the letter, slipped it back into the envelope, and shook her head. "She's only twenty-one, Anna. She can't possibly be ready for missionary work. And in China! It is so far away, and mission work requires a lifetime contract. I worry that she doesn't know what she has gotten herself into."

Anna studied Lottie. "Are you sure it is truly Eddie you are thinking of?"

"What do you mean?" Lottie asked, defensive heat rising in her chest.

"Well," Anna replied carefully, "I know you have shared your desire to do mission work in China. Could it be you are jealous that Eddie gets to go instead of you?"

"That's not it at all," Lottie snapped, grabbing her hat and wrap. "You're wrong, Anna."

Lottie stepped outside into the early April sunshine and strode down the muddy streets of Cartersville. A shower had just passed through, and the freshness of the air seeped into Lottie's soul. As usual, Anna knew her too well. Lottie felt a stomach-wrenching mix of jealousy, fear for Eddie, and excitement at the doors that were opening. As she walked, Lottie silently prayed, wondering what God was trying to tell her through the surprising news of Eddie's impending departure.

Lottie traveled to Viewmont to help Eddie prepare for her journey. The sisters spent many long hours talking about the changes in society and the transitions within the Southern Baptist leadership. They also pondered the new doors that were opening for women.

"You'll be by my side before you know it," Eddie insisted one late spring evening as they packed her final trunk.

"I don't know. We have so much left to do in Cartersville."

Eddie rolled her eyes and shook her head. "Anyone can do the work in Cartersville, Lottie. God needs you in China. You're a natural at learning difficult languages, and the Chinese dialects are some of the hardest in the world."

Lottie silently continued layering neatly folded linens in the trunk. She couldn't deny the tugging on her heart that had strengthened over the past few weeks. But she was not as young or impulsive as Eddie.

She was thirty-one years old and far too responsible to rush into a major life decision like missionary work.

Eddie laughed at Lottie's somber silence. "I know you, Lottie Moon," she said. "Mark my words—within a year you'll be headed to China."

Eddie arrived in China in June 1872, and her letters soon regaled Lottie with detailed descriptions of the sights, sounds, and smells of the treaty port of Tengchow where she lived. By January 1873, Lottie could not take it anymore. She wrote to H.A. Tupper, head of the Foreign Missions Board, asking how she might be approved by the board as a single female missionary to China. Her friend, Anna Safford, was a member of a different type of church, but she also felt drawn to mission work in China. The two ladies waited and prayed together, both hoping for board approval to follow God's leading to a far away land.

After weeks of agonizing anticipation, both Lottie and Anna received word they would be sent as missionaries as soon as they could make preparations. On June 12, 1873, at the graduation ceremony for the Cartersville Female High School, Lottie and Anna said goodbye to their students, friends, and the community that loved them. Tears and well wishes mingled in an emotional day laced with love and laughter and memories. Within days, Lottie was ready to begin a new chapter of her life. She bid Anna a warm and wistful goodbye with a promise to try to reconnect someday in China.

On July 7, Lottie Moon became an official missionary to China for the Southern Baptist Foreign Mission Board. She had no doubts about her decision, and even though the future was uncertain, she had few fears. Lottie knew she was finally doing what God designed her to do, and she was enthusiastic and energized for the road ahead. She could hardly wait to join Eddie in China.

Before she left, Lottie visited her old home at Viewmont. She said goodbye to her brother Ike and his wife, as well as countless other relatives and friends in the area. Then Lottie headed to the Alabama-Tennessee border, where Orie and her husband John lived with their six little boys. As they sat on the wide porch drinking sweet tea and watching the boys play in the yard, Lottie and Orie talked happily about their younger years.

"Oh, what wayward souls we were!" Orie cried with a laugh. "We were so sure of ourselves. We had no need for God or men."

Lottie laughed too. "We certainly were strong-minded and thick-headed."

"Now look at us," Orie said. "We thought we didn't need God, and you're giving your life to go serve Him in China. We thought we didn't need men, and I'm married and raising six little men of my own. How life changes!"

The sisters sat in silence, enjoying the warmth of the summer sunshine. Then Orie turned to Lottie, warm tears in her eyes, but a smile playing on her lips.

"I will miss you, Lottie. But I am so proud of you. And Mama and Papa would be proud too."

Lottie swallowed hard as tears pricked at her eyelids. Her sister's approval meant so much to her. She knew she was making the right decision, leaving everything she knew to minister in China, but it was good to hear Orie say it out loud.

Before she left Alabama, Lottie wrote an article for the *Religious Herald* expressing her excitement for her upcoming ministry in China.

"Could a Christian woman possibly desire higher honor than to be permitted to go from house to house and tell of a Savior to those who have never heard His name?" she wrote. "We could not conceive a life which would more thoroughly satisfy the mind and heart of a true follower of the Lord Jesus."

Her thoughts shared and her goodbyes complete, Lottie felt ready to go. On August 15, 1873, she boarded a train in Florence, Alabama. She was headed to New York, then on to San Francisco. There she would board a ship bound for China. Lottie was enthralled, eager, and excited to let the adventure begin!

To the Edge of the World and Beyond

Lottie's train rolled endlessly across the American landscape. She watched the green hills of Appalachia turn to the golden plains of the Midwest. Then the train climbed haltingly through the majestic violet-blue peaks of the Rocky Mountains. Finally, travel-weary and motion sick, Lottie climbed off the train into the foggy bustle of San Francisco. She took a deep breath of the fresh sea air, tinged with salty, fishy aromas. She was immensely glad the train trip was over.

In San Francisco, Lottie stayed with A.S. Worrell and his family, old friends from Lottie's days at the Danville Female Academy. They spent many pleasant days exploring the city and many long evenings debating and discussing around the crackling fire.

"You've wanted to go to China for some time, haven't you?" A.S. Worrell asked Lottie one evening. "I seem to recall you speaking about it, even back in the Danville days."

Lottie smiled. "Those days seem so long ago! In truth, going to China is a desire God put in my heart many, many years ago—long before my sister left."

"I'm sure people think you are simply going to chaperone her …"

"They are welcome to think that," Lottie retorted. "But they are wrong. I want to share the Jesus I love so much with those who have never heard His name."

"Are you afraid?" Mrs. Worrell asked.

Lottie thought for a moment. "No. Not afraid. Only a bit anxious to get started. In some ways, going to China feels like going home, even though it is to a home I've never known before."

A.S. Worrell smiled. "Your spirit is remarkable, Lottie, and your sacrifice is admirable. Our prayers will be with you. I have no doubt that God will accomplish great things through you in China."

On September 1, 1873, Lottie boarded the Costa Rica, and at high noon, they sailed out into the sun-kissed Pacific Ocean, headed for China. There were several other missionaries on board, and Lottie was never at a loss for good company. While many of the others struggled with sadness over all they had left behind, Lottie only struggled with overwhelming seasickness that set in on the first day of the long voyage. She struggled to eat and often found herself hanging over the ship's rail, counting on the cool, fresh sea breezes to bring relief from the endless nausea. She rejoiced when the Costa Rica docked in Yokohama, Japan on September 25th. After more than three weeks at sea, Lottie wanted to kiss the dry land as she stepped off the boat!

Local English-speakers were happy to help Lottie explore Japan a bit while the ship was in port. She loved the little shops with their slippery silks and intricate carvings. At the next two stops—in Kobe and Nagasaki—local missionaries toured Lottie through Japanese gardens and shrines, showing her the exquisite beauty of the country. Lottie loved every minute, but she found herself growing restless. She longed to move on to China to start the mission work God had for her.

Finally the ship left Nagasaki, bound for Shanghai, China. But what should have been a pleasant forty-eight-hour journey soon turned into a nightmare. On the first night at sea, Lottie awoke to the violent tossing of the ship. She could hear the wind howling and glass shattering.

"What's going on?" Lottie asked a crewman as he hurried past her cabin.

"Hurricane, Ma'am," he snapped. Then his voice softened a bit. "You'd best hang on. Looks like we're in for a rough time of it."

Lottie spent the night huddled in her cabin, listening to pieces of the deck break away around her. By morning, the storm had worsened, and the ship had lost its rudder. They were drifting aimlessly, out of control, tossed like a small toy across the raging waves. The hopeless, helpless passengers gathered together.

"We are going to die," lamented one of the other missionaries. "We have not even begun our mission work, and now it is going to end!"

Lottie had a different perspective. "We must trust that God is in control of this storm."

"How can you be so calm?" another passenger asked.

A peaceful look passed over Lottie's face. "I have no doubts that my Jesus is with us. In fact, I would not be the least bit surprised to look out and see a figure walking across the wild water, saying, 'It is I; be not afraid.'"

Lottie's faith proved sound, and when the hurricane had passed, the Costa Rica was able to limp back into the Japanese port of Nagasaki. After a few days in port, they were headed for Shanghai again—this time with much greater success.

Lottie Moon arrived in China on October 7, 1873. She was greeted by the Crawfords, the missionaries from Tengchow who were hosting Eddie. Lottie liked them immediately, and although Eddie had stayed behind in Tengchow, Lottie felt she was among family. She peppered the Crawfords with questions about life and work in China, and she readily absorbed every word of their answers.

The journey to China had been long and difficult, with storms and obstacles all along the way. Lottie felt she had finally reached her proper destination, where she was truly meant to be. Little did Lottie know, her journey and ministry in China would prove a much wilder ride than her journey to China had ever been!

Evangelistic Excursion

As Lottie ventured into the city of Shanghai, the Chinese culture assaulted her senses. Pungent, oily, spicy scents tickled her nostrils and turned her sensitive stomach. The harsh, almost guttural tones of the Chinese language with its choppy flow and abrupt inflection tangled in her untrained ears. Donkeys and children and carts and merchants mingled chaotically in the crowded streets. It was an overwhelming feast for Lottie's eager mind and heart.

After a brief stay in Shanghai, Mrs. Crawford and Lottie boarded another ship to sail to Chefoo in the Shantung Province, only fifty-five miles from Lottie's new home in Tengchow. They left Mr. Crawford behind on business, and Lottie was overjoyed to be starting the final leg of her journey. As the ship docked in Chefoo, Lottie surveyed the wide fields that rolled away to where craggy mountain peaks touched the sky at the horizon. Shantung Province was rumored to be the most densely populated place on earth, and Lottie was about to join the millions who already lived there.

After a few days in Chefoo, Mrs. Crawford told Lottie they were ready to go on to Tengchow. "We will travel in shentzes," she told Lottie. "It's the easiest way to handle these long journeys."

Lottie looked skeptically at the shentzes that pulled up to the gate. They looked like wide-mouthed baskets lying on their sides. Each was mounted on two poles that were attached to a mule at the front and a mule in the back. A Chinese escort stood beside each shentze.

"How does one ride in a shentze?" Lottie asked hesitantly.

"You climb inside the basket and lean back on the pillows," Mrs. Crawford instructed, demonstrating in one of the shentzes. "Then a thick curtain is pulled over the mouth of the basket to block the weather, dust, and prying eyes."

Lottie was unconvinced that a shentze was the best form of travel, but she was ready to give it a try. With a shrug of her shoulders, Lottie climbed into her shentze and they were off. After two days and fifty-five miles of traveling, Lottie was sure there must be a better mode of transportation. Every joint in her body ached with inactivity. Every muscle felt bruised from the bumpy ride. But she was finally at the Crawfords' compound in Tengchow.

"Lottie!" Eddie cried, her face shining with pure joy.

Lottie climbed stiffly from the shentze and fell into Eddie's waiting arms. The sisters clung to each other for a long time, intensely happy to be together again.

"I told you that you would be in China in less than a year," Eddie teased through her happy tears.

Lottie laughed out loud, wiping away a few tears of her own. It was so good to be with Eddie in the place

God had put in her heart so long ago. The puzzle pieces of her life seemed to finally be coming together into a perfect picture.

Lottie's first task was to tackle the tricky Chinese language. The official language in Tengchow was Mandarin, but as the foreign words swirled around her tired ears, Lottie quickly discovered that few people spoke true Mandarin. Many dialects were used throughout the region, and Lottie wanted to have at least a basic grasp of each one. She worked hard with a tutor every day, but she found the difficult dialects much harder than any of the other languages she had learned.

Life was not all work and study for Lottie. She got out to explore the city and meet other missionaries and Chinese believers. The city was surrounded by a thick wall and filled with small, one-level homes built in long rows, and each home was surrounded by its own wall. The streets were narrow and crafted from bumpy, worn out millstones. Nearly 80,000 people were packed into the crowded city.

Some of the members of the Crawfords' church— Monument Street Baptist Church—visited Lottie to welcome her to China. Of all the people she met, one of Lottie's favorite people was missionary Sallie Holmes. Sallie had come to China with her husband many years before Lottie arrived. When Sallie was pregnant with their son, her husband was murdered by bandits. Sallie thought about moving back to the United States, but she loved the Chinese people too much. She wanted to continue sharing Jesus with them. So she stayed and raised her little boy, Landrum, while she ran a girls' boarding school and made frequent trips to outlying villages to do evangelistic work.

Lottie was intrigued and inspired by Sallie's plucky spirit and love for China. So she was thrilled when Sallie showed up on the doorstep of the Crawfords' house with a picnic basket and a wide grin. As Sallie entered the room, she and Mrs. Crawford exchanged meaningful glances.

"Today we are going on a picnic," she announced.

"Who will be coming?" Lottie wondered out loud.

"Eddie, Mrs. Crawford, you, and me. And a deacon from the church will come as a chaperone."

Lottie was mildly suspicious. In just three weeks in China, she had come to know that gleam in Sallie's eye.

"Are we just going on a picnic?" she asked.

"Well…we might do a little evangelism too," Sallie admitted.

That turned out to be quite an understatement! From the first village the women entered, throngs of bright-faced children surrounded them, staring with wide, dark eyes. Men also clamored to listen to the words of the foreigners, but the women of the villages hung back shyly and observed from a distance. The Chinese deacon shared his testimony with the men, and the four missionary women ministered to the ladies and children. Lottie listened patiently as the still-unfamiliar Chinese words swirled around her. She tried to recognize words she had heard before, but most of them were still beyond her understanding.

They stayed in each village for a while, and then moved on to a new village where the scene was repeated. This continued until the sun was high in the sky. When they finally settled down for lunch near a rural village, they drew an even bigger crowd. The villagers were fascinated by the forks and knives the women were using, and they seemed especially fascinated by Lottie. They poked and prodded her and shouted questions at her. Eddie translated the questions.

"How old are you? Are you married? Why did you come here? Do you have a mother-in-law?"

Lottie patiently answered each question through Eddie, laughing at some of the inquiries. When lunch was over, they taught a hymn to the children and shared a simple gospel message. Then they moved on to the next village.

This pattern continued throughout the afternoon. As the sun melted into the mountains, the little caravan headed for home. Lottie was exhausted, but exhilarated. She knew she was doing exactly what God wanted her to do. She just wished she knew the language better so she could be a more active participant in the ministry.

As they traveled home, Sallie glanced over at Lottie. "Mission accomplished," she said with a grin. "But tomorrow is a new day with a new mission."

Lottie looked out across the landscape of Shantung Province, stretching far and wide and dotted with villages and cities and farms. As long as she was in China, every day would bring a new mission, and Lottie wondered if the work would ever be done.

Mrs. Lan's Missionfield

"Lottie! Lottie! You'll never believe what happened!"

Eddie rushed into Lottie's room, her eyes burning with excitement. Lottie looked up from her writing desk with alarm.

"Is something wrong?"

Eddie shook her head as she struggled to pull a suitcase from beneath Lottie's bed. "No, no. Nothing is wrong. Something is right! Can I borrow this suitcase?"

"Of course," Lottie said. "But where are you going?"

"You know Mrs. Lan from church, right?"

Lottie nodded. Mrs. Lan was one of only a handful of faithful women at the Monument Street Baptist Church. Her children also attended the schools that were run by Mrs. Crawford and Sallie Holmes.

"Well, a few days ago, Mrs. Lan went back to her home town to celebrate Chinese New Year," Eddie went on. "She just sent word that she was sharing her faith with some family and friends, and suddenly the whole village wants to know about Jesus! She has taught them all the hymns and scripture she knows, but there are still so many questions. She is begging for our help!"

"Are you going alone?"

"No," Eddie said. "Sallie Holmes is coming with me. Can you imagine it? People are eager to hear! This is what we've prayed for."

"Can I come?"

Eddie's excitement dimmed slightly, and she paused before she spoke. "Lottie, you've only been here a few months, and you are still learning the language and culture. I just fear that…"

Lottie swallowed her disappointment and forced a smile to her face. "You're right. I would slow you down. I'll stay here and help Mrs. Crawford. And I will pray for you and your work."

Eddie gave Lottie an affectionate squeeze. "Thank you for understanding."

By noon, Eddie and Sallie had started for the village, eight miles away. But they soon found the work was more than even they could handle. So they called for Mrs. Crawford, Lottie, and another missionary to join them. Lottie was ecstatic!

When they reached the village, the missionary women were surprised to find the villagers huddled in small groups, studying scriptures, singing hymns, and discussing the gospel message.

"These people are literally hungering and thirsting after righteousness," Lottie observed. "They are drinking in every bit of hope and doctrine they are given!"

There were tears in Mrs. Crawford's eyes as she looked out over the village. "We have never seen such a response—not in all our years in China!"

The women immediately got to work. They organized classes and taught lessons to the new believers. Within days, nearly everyone in the village believed in Jesus. At night, the exhausted women slept in Mrs. Lan's family home on a kang, a traditional Chinese platform bed that was made of mud bricks and heated with warm air from the central stove. Even topped with a thin pad, kangs were not particularly comfortable, as they were hard as rocks and often unbearably hot. Thankfully, the missionaries were too tired to care.

After a few exhausting—but thrilling—days in the village, Mrs. Crawford, Sallie Holmes, and the other missionary woman needed to return to their regular responsibilities in Tengchow. They decided to leave Lottie and Eddie with Mrs. Lan to finish the work.

"But I barely speak the language," Lottie protested, panic rising in her chest. "What if something comes up that we can't handle?"

Sallie laughed at the fear in Lottie's face. "You've done well this week, Lottie. And it's just a few more days. You'll be fine."

"Besides," Mrs. Crawford reminded her, "Eddie is very capable, and Mrs. Lan is here to help. And I will send Mr. Mung to preach at the church service on Sunday."

Lottie fought back a wave of loneliness as Mrs. Crawford and the other missionary climbed into shentzes and Sallie swung onto the back of her donkey.

When they were gone, Lottie hurried back to help Eddie. She was determined to learn all she could and help as much as possible.

The days flew by and Sunday dawned, bright and beautiful. Mr. Mung, a deacon from Tengchow, arrived and was ready to preach the sermon. A Chinese Christian girl volunteered to lead the singing, and the service went smoothly. Many of the townspeople came, their faces radiant with the joy of their new beliefs. A new church had been established, and Mrs. Lan agreed to stay in the village for a while to help the church grow.

On Monday morning, Lottie and Eddie climbed into open sedan chairs—seats that were carried on poles by Chinese porters. The chairs were more comfortable than shentzes, even though they were more exposed. The happy sisters waved goodbye to their new friends in the village. Then they exchanged grins and settled back for the long ride home. What an adventure the past week had been!

As Lottie and Eddie traveled home in tired silence, a cold, wet wind blew in from the sea. It wrapped itself around Lottie and burrowed into her bones, chilling her entire body. She glanced over at her little sister. Eddie was shivering. The open sedan chairs offered no relief from the weather, and Lottie and Eddie were only wearing light shawls. Lottie felt a rush of thankfulness flood through her as she stepped into the Crawfords' house in Tengchow.

Lottie changed into warm clothes and snuggled under her blankets, sinking into the softness. It felt so good to be in a real bed after a week of sleeping on a kang. As she drifted off to sleep, Lottie could hear Eddie coughing in the next room. By the time they had arrived in Tengchow, Eddie had been feeling very sick. Barely able to walk, she had gone straight to her room. Lottie had not been concerned, because she understood how tired Eddie was. But the cough sounded bad, even from the next room. Lottie wondered if the strain of the week and the stress of the trip had been too much for her sister. Would Eddie be all right?

Setbacks and Struggles

Eddie was not all right. The hacking cough and fever developed into typhoid pneumonia. She spent long weeks in bed, and Lottie was right by her side, gently nursing her back to health.

During the quiet days with Eddie, Lottie had a lot of time to think about how God wanted to use her in China. There were two elements of the Chinese culture that truly broke Lottie's heart, and they both involved the beautiful young Chinese girls. She spent hours wondering how she could lovingly show the people that God could free them from traditions that had endured for generations.

The first thing that troubled Lottie was the ancient practice of foot binding. When a Chinese girl was barely more than a baby, her toes were bent backward, underneath her foot. The feet were then bent in half until the soft bones broke and the little girl screamed in pain. Then the feet were tightly bound in the broken, folded position with long strips of stiff cloth. Every day—or every few days—the feet were bent a little further and bound again, the cloths wrapped tighter and tighter each time. Often, the feet were repeatedly broken until the desired size and shape were attained.

Once binding began, a little girl could never again run and skip and play. They hobbled from place to place, trying to keep up with the work in spite of agonizing pain. But tiny feet were considered beautiful, and they would help a girl attract a rich and successful husband someday. Mothers would try to keep their daughters' feet under three inches, considered the ideal foot size. Lottie was heartbroken each time she saw a tiny girl tottering along with sadness in her eyes.

The other thing that bothered Lottie was the lack of educational opportunities for girls. Most girls never attended school, and very few ever learned to read. Education was reserved for boys and a handful of upper class girls.

Once they were married, girls went to live in the home of their mother-in-law. Many mothers-in-law were cruel and made unreasonable demands on their sons' wives. Young girls were often beaten or even killed when they couldn't live up to the expectations of the mother-in-law, the most powerful figure in the family. Their spirits were bound and broken, just like their tiny feet, and Lottie longed to offer them freedom through Jesus Christ.

These concerns constantly danced in Lottie's mind, but concern for Eddie rose to the forefront. Even when Eddie's body began to heal, she was tired and irritated all the time. Sadness and hopelessness were woven throughout her days. She began overseeing the school and taking on some of her other routine duties again, but her joyful, enthusiastic spirit was eclipsed by persistent depression.

"Eddie, what's wrong?" Lottie asked in desperation one afternoon.

"What do you mean?" Eddie snapped.

Lottie sighed. "I feel like I've lost my little sister."

Tears came like a flood. "I don't even know what's happening to me anymore," Eddie admitted. "I'm always tired and frustrated and angry. No matter how hard I try, I just can't get away from my sadness."

Lottie hated seeing Eddie so despondent and listless. She wrote to the churches in the United States asking for money so the sisters could have a house of their own. Lottie hoped being away from Mr. Crawford's domineering personality and the stress of a shared living situation would help Eddie find peace and stability. But nothing seemed to help.

Lottie was doing all of her ministry work plus most of Eddie's work. She was visiting homes in the city, traveling to rural villages with Sallie, teaching Sunday school, and serving as the administrator and head teacher in the school Eddie oversaw. At the end of each day, Lottie was exhausted, and often a bit frustrated and irritable. She often felt she was so busy she was actually accomplishing nothing.

In late 1874, Lottie was finally too worn out to continue the feverish pace of her life. She became ill, and she and Eddie were ordered by the other missionaries to go see an American doctor in Chefoo. The doctor ordered the sisters to Shanghai for a few months of rest. Lottie was thrilled, because she knew she needed the rest, and she also knew her old friend, Anna Safford, lived nearby. Lottie hoped they would have plenty of time to visit and reconnect with each other.

After some rest and relaxation—and good fellowship with Anna—Lottie felt recharged, ready to take on the world again. She couldn't wait to get back to Tengchow and back to work. But Eddie did not reflect Lottie's recovery. She was still sad, angry, listless, and depressed. Lottie was at a loss. She didn't know what else to do for her once-vibrant little sister.

While Eddie closed herself away in the house and refused to see or speak with anyone, Lottie tackled her ministry opportunities head-on. In addition to keeping a watchful eye on the school, Lottie became Sallie Holmes' permanent traveling partner, visiting villages throughout the region and sharing Jesus with those who had never heard. Although she didn't enjoy the inevitable poking and prodding from the children, and pestering with questions from the adults, Lottie did love the dynamic, active nature of the ministry. The trips with Sallie soon became something Lottie eagerly anticipated.

"Are you up for a long trip with me?" Sallie asked when she stopped by one afternoon.

Lottie sipped her tea. "What did you have in mind?"

"Eleven days and more than forty villages. Are you up for it?"

Lottie thought about all her responsibilities in Tengchow. But then the dark, searching eyes and eager, open smiles of the villagers flashed through her mind. She knew what she needed to do.

"I'm always up for a trip with you!"

When they reached their initial destination, Lottie and Sallie found the accommodations that had been made for them were in a priest's house on old temple grounds. The house was nice enough, with a tile roof, dirt floor, paper-covered windows, and a concrete kang. But the front yard was full of stone idols with blank eyes and evil grins. Lottie shuddered every time she passed them, but they reminded her heart how lost the people really were, trusting in stone to protect and guide them.

Using the house as a headquarters, Lottie and Sallie reached out to the village. People came at all hours of the day and night to hear the missionary ladies tell the story of Jesus. Long after the sun had set, candlelight flickered on the faces longing to hear and understand more about a God who loved them. The scene repeated itself again and again throughout their journey. Huge crowds gathered, and the missionaries spoke until their throats were cracked and dry. Then they would fall asleep on the kang, swaddled in smoky, stifling heat and surrounded by the crackle of crawling insects.

"Are you as tired as I am?" Sallie asked wearily as they traveled home to Tengchow.

Lottie groaned. "Every bone in my body aches with exhaustion. I think that was our longest trip ever."

"Forty-four villages," Sallie agreed. "But think how many people heard God's good news."

They rode in silence for a few minutes as faces from the past eleven days danced through their memories. Finally, Lottie broke the silence.

"It's a good kind of tired."

Sallie nodded. "The best kind there is."

When Lottie got home, she found Eddie worse than ever before. Over the next several months, it became increasingly clear that Eddie could not stay in China. In October 1876, Lottie sent Eddie to Japan with Mrs. Yates, a missionary from Shanghai. Lottie hoped the beauty and more temperate climate of Japan would soothe Eddie's nerves, heal her body, and lift her spirits. But within days of their arrival in Japan, Mrs. Yates sent frantic word to Lottie. She said Eddie had taken a turn for the worse, and Lottie needed to come at once.

Within four hours, Lottie was packed and headed toward Nagasaki, Japan. When she saw Eddie, pangs of heartbreak stabbed through Lottie's broken heart. This was not the bright, beautiful, lively Eddie of Lottie's memory. Before her stood a broken, hopeless girl, sick in both body and spirit. Overcome with grief, Lottie swallowed the tears that crowded her throat and pulled Eddie into her arms.

Eddie began to cry, curling into Lottie like a little girl. "Oh, Lottie! I can't do this anymore. I just can't!"

Lottie reached up and stroked Eddie's hair, transported for a moment to an earlier, simpler time. Lottie knew what she had to do, and with a deep sigh she admitted it out loud for the first time.

"I know, sweet Eddie. I know. And that is why I have come to take you home."

"To Tengchow?"

"No, Eddie. To Virginia. It's time for you to go home to Virginia."

Lottie and Eddie arrived at Viewmont on December 22, 1876. Orie and John were living there with their six sons, and Isaac and Mag lived nearby. Mollie had recently died, but her husband and daughter came from Norfolk, and Colie came from Washington D.C. where she worked at the Treasury Department. They all spent a chaotic and joyful Christmas together, and the combination of family and medicine seemed to transform Eddie. The shadows were gone and the joy was dawning on her face again. Lottie knew she had made the right decision.

When she was sure Eddie was on the mend, Lottie reluctantly left her family and toured the South, speaking in churches, at conventions and ladies' luncheons, and anywhere else people would listen. She vividly painted word pictures of life in China and the desperate need for more workers to feed the hungry hearts. Lottie made pleas for workers, supplies, and funding. And wherever she spoke, people listened.

Finally, Lottie made one last trip to Viewmont. After saying a tearful goodbye to her siblings, Lottie found Eddie on the wide front porch.

"I'm leaving, Eddie. China needs me, and I've been here long enough."

Eddie looked at Lottie with pleading eyes. "I wish I could go with you. Will you love for me, Lottie? Will you promise to love them?"

Lottie reached out and squeezed Eddie's hand. "With all my heart."

On November 8, 1877, Lottie sailed for China. She wondered if the people of Tengchow would remember her. Would they welcome her back? Or would she be just another "foreign devil" to them once again?

The Challenge of Change

As she traveled back toward China, Lottie's excitement swelled. During a brief stop in Japan, Lottie posted a letter to her old friend, H.A. Tupper, head of the Foreign Mission Board.

"Now I honestly believe that I love China the best," she wrote. "Actually, which is stranger still, I love the Chinese best."

Many things had changed since Lottie first arrived in China in 1873. Thirteen new missionaries had arrived, and new approaches to ministry were being tried and tested in China. When Lottie arrived in Shanghai, Mrs. Yates was bubbling over with news. While Lottie was away, the first General Conference of Missionaries in China was held. Many missionaries from all regions of China were in attendance. They made friendships, exchanged ideas, and proposed new plans for reaching China with the gospel.

During the conference, the missionary wives and single female missionaries had come together to form a Women's Missionary Association. Mrs. Yates was elected president, and Lottie's dear friend Anna Safford was the vice president.

"It's so exciting!" Mrs. Yates gushed. "It's an opportunity for us to band together as women to make a difference."

"It sounds wonderful," Lottie agreed. "Perhaps we can also share ideas and techniques for working with women and children."

"Exactly! And we even have a women's magazine planned." Mrs. Yates paused. "Actually, we wanted to ask you to be a contributing editor."

"I'd love to!"

Mrs. Yates sighed with relief. "I'm so glad. We have such big plans. We could definitely use your help!"

After a brief stay in Shanghai, Lottie sailed on to Chefoo. It was December, and she arrived in a blustery snowstorm. The missionaries in Chefoo urged Lottie to wait out the storm, but she was determined to get back to "her people" in Tengchow. Lottie wrapped herself in layers and layers of clothing until she was almost as round as a snowman. Then she waddled her way to a waiting shentze and climbed in. She was determined to get to Tengchow as soon as possible.

Lottie arrived in Tengchow to swirling snow and a warm welcome. The people remembered her and expressed sincere gratitude for her return. When the weather cleared and Lottie was able to venture to the villages, she met with the same response. It seemed the fiery little Miss Moon was not easily forgotten!

Fall and winter of 1877 had brought rampant famine to the region. The rural areas were particularly hard hit, and villagers flocked to cities like Tengchow looking for food, work, and shelter. The churches in Tengchow were reaching out to rural people in new ways. Challenge had brought a connectivity not seen before in the city, and there was an open-minded spirit in the face of this change. Tengchow was perfectly set for Lottie's long-time dream of starting a boarding school for girls.

The school opened in February 1878 with only five girls. Soon the number had grown to thirteen. Lottie became rapidly frustrated, however, by how difficult it was to recruit, enroll, and retain her female students. The main duties of a girl in China were having her feet bound, learning household tasks, marrying young and well, and working as a virtual slave to her mother-in-law. Members of the upper class were especially bound by these traditions.

In a desperate attempt to increase enrollment, Lottie personally assumed financial responsibility for all of her students. Not only did she waive tuition costs, Lottie herself paid for food and lodging for every girl at her school. Even with such sacrificial provisions, most Chinese refused to educate their daughters. They simply didn't see any reason for girls to have education. Lottie's school was primarily comprised of girls who had been rescued from abuse and neglect and needed a home.

The school dormitory was a row of rooms in Lottie's house. Each room had a large kang that could sleep up to five girls. Students were fed three meals each day, but Lottie didn't eat most of the traditional Chinese foods, so she had no idea what the girls were being fed. As it turned out, the cook Lottie hired was awful, and several girls left the school just because the food was inedible! Those who stayed had daily lessons in reading, math, geography, and singing.

Schools operated differently in China, and Lottie had to adapt to the local customs. They learned everything by memorization, and they recited their memorized lessons with their backs to the teacher as a sign of respect. When Lottie came into a classroom, she was offered special respect as a headmistress. Students would immediately turn their backs to her and shout their lessons as loudly as they could. It took Lottie some time to adjust to the volume, but she was impressed by the girls' ability to learn—many could soon recite the entire books of Matthew and Mark from the New Testament!

Lottie had dreamed that education would bring an end to foot binding and young marriage. She had hoped it would foster harmony, enlightenment, and opportunities to share Jesus. But she found the traditions were deeply ingrained in the culture and would not be so easily broken as she had at first believed. She fought and spoke against the things that troubled her, but most of her words fell on deaf ears. Girls were afraid of angering their families, and families were afraid of jeopardizing a good marriage match. The people resisted change, even as they began to understand why it was necessary.

Running the school was much more challenging than Lottie had ever imagined. Despite her best efforts, the girls often fought with each other. And when she wasn't busy separating bickering girls, Lottie was battling dirt, bugs, germs, and rodents. In spite of the constant stress and strain, however, Lottie loved and believed in her girls. She saw potential in every one of them. She cared for them like they were her own daughters, and they loved her back. Lottie even took in a sickly five-year-old girl, much younger than her other students, because the child's mother had abandoned her. Lottie nursed and nurtured the little girl until she was thriving, and then she sent word to the mother that the child had been cured by love.

Lottie felt love could cure just about any ill she encountered. Her life was busy, hectic, and challenging, but it was also exhilarating to see lives changing and culture transforming. Lottie always felt there was more she should be doing, so much more that needed to be done. It frustrated her that while she worked in China, her fellow Christians in the United States seemed oblivious to the need that existed around the world. Lottie saw them as stingy in their giving and averse to self-sacrifice. How could she help them understand the need? How could she encourage them to get involved?

For the Record

In between village adventures and schoolroom escapades, Lottie started using her gift of words to influence the world. She wrote letters requesting financial and emotional support for the missionaries in China. She wrote reports detailing the many ministries that were operating among the Chinese people. She wrote articles documenting the reality of the conditions and needs in China. Her words became a battle cry in churches across the South and beyond.

As much as Lottie wrote, she also read widely. It often took many months for American magazines and letters to reach Lottie in Tengchow, but when they arrived, she devoured them with her eyes, her mind, and her heart. Even if the information was a bit outdated, Lottie was always hungry to know more and broaden her window on the world.

After one particularly difficult trip to rural villages, Lottie came home to a new copy of one of her favorite magazines, the *Biblical Recorder*. One of the featured articles was on mission work, and the author proudly proclaimed the days of missionary hardship were over.

"What?" Lottie fumed, slapping the magazine down in disgust. "Absurd! Clearly, this man has never lived the life of a missionary. If he only knew a fraction of the things we experience every day …"

She hurried for her pen, ink, and paper. Sitting at her writing desk, tense with indignant energy, Lottie wrote a lengthy rebuttal to the rosy article. Her pen danced across the page, detailing the challenges of her latest village trip with Sallie. Lottie wrote about the crowded, smoky, stuffy rooms with dirt floors and concrete beds. She described the poking and prodding and endless questioning that nearly drove her crazy. She told about the hatred missionaries often faced and the death threats that were hurled at "foreign devils." With eloquent, expressive words, Lottie made it clear that physical, psychological, and spiritual hardships were still very much a part of modern missionary life. Lottie's rebuttal was published in the magazine, and made waves in the sleepy Southern Baptist society.

As if to illustrate Lottie's claims, she and Sallie undertook a grueling trip near the end of 1878. The plan was to visit as many villages as possible. From the very first stop, people thronged the two ladies. They pressed against their donkeys and pulled on their skirts. Lottie taught the women and girls, and Sallie taught the men as they travelled from village to village. The first day they made several stops and were still alive with excitement as the sun slipped behind the hills.

When they arrived at their pre-planned sleeping quarters for the night, Lottie and Sallie were exhausted and longing for rest. But people from the village surged into the cramped bedroom. They climbed onto the kang and squeezed into every bare spot on the well-swept dirt floor. Then they turned eager eyes on Lottie and Sallie, ready for the message they had to proclaim.

With cracked, dry throats and voices barely above a whisper, Lottie and Sallie took turns sharing God's message with the people. In the wee hours of the morning, they were finally able to herd the villagers gently from the room. Sallie stretched a shawl across the narrow doorway and collapsed on the kang. Within minutes, both women were lost in deep sleep.

The privacy and peace were short-lived. By the time the missionaries awoke, just after dawn, the villagers were already waiting on the other side of the shawl. Before starting to teach, Lottie and Sallie ate a simple breakfast of millet. Thirty sets of curious eyes watched their every move. Lottie felt exposed and annoyed and frustrated. She was still tired from the previous day, and she just wanted a few minutes alone. In exasperation, she turned to an old woman who was squeezed against her on the kang.

"Do you realize there are thirty people watching us?" Lottie asked brusquely. "They are watching us eat. What can they possibly want to see?"

The old lady dropped her gaze in shame. When she looked up, apologetic tears hovered on the rims of her eyelids.

"Forgive us," she said softly. "We have never seen any heavenly people before."

Lottie swallowed hard as the millet stuck in her throat. She was instantly ashamed of her selfish perspective. The villagers saw her as a representation of Jesus, and Lottie wasn't sure she was doing a very good job representing Him. She smiled warmly at the old woman, and she was greeted with a brilliant grin in return. Lottie resolved she would do a better job representing her Lord and Savior. She was often disturbed by the constant touching and endless questions, and she knew she could be impatient and abrupt.

"I need to conquer my unwillingness to talk and be fingered," Lottie wrote, "and I need to teach the children."

Lottie decided she needed to focus on the positive things she found as she ministered. In her writings, she wanted to clearly and accurately portray the obstacles while simultaneously emphasizing God's glory and goodness. After one long, hard day, Lottie struggled to find something positive to write. As she lay back on the kang with a deep sigh, a glimmer in the corner caught her eye. She popped up and grabbed her writing supplies.

"There are beautiful spider webs on the rafters," she wrote, "and clean matting on the kang."

Lottie began to actively try to find beauty in the world that surrounded her, but she didn't want to minimize the challenges either. She wanted her friends in the United States to fully understand her need for their prayers and support. In a letter to H.A. Tupper and the Foreign Mission Board, Lottie detailed the sheer fatigue that came from traveling and speaking up to a dozen times a day. She recounted the uncomfortable accommodations, starving and unwashed people, nauseating smells and sights, and rampant disease.

Regarding the reality of hardships, Lottie closed her letter by pointing out, "A few days of roughing it as we ladies do habitually will convince the most skeptical."

Lottie also wrote many letters explaining the need for furloughs—or rest periods—for the missionaries in China. She repeatedly chided the Southern Baptists in the United States, who numbered over a million in 1878, for sending so few missionaries to reach over 30 million Chinese people. She begged for funds and, above all, more workers to get the job done.

Although her letters and articles were impassioned and her energy seemed endless, Lottie sometimes struggled with deep loneliness and a sense of hopelessness at the enormity of her mission. During these times, when her heart was low, Lottie read and re-read her Bible, devotional books, and encouraging letters from her old friends. God always used these little lights to lift her spirits and re-energize Lottie for the work He had for her to do.

She wrote to her friends in Cartersville, "Your prayers help us bear up against the depressing influences around us."

Even in her lowest moments, Lottie never doubted God's love, presence or power. In fact, in her private journal, she noted, "As I wander from village to village, I feel it is no idle fancy that the Master walks beside me and I hear His voice saying gently, 'I am with you always, even unto the end.'"

But just as Lottie's heart was finding a home on the path of peace, change was coming to China, and Lottie's ministry was about to take a new direction.

A New Network

In September 1881, Lottie's ministry changed dramatically when Sallie Holmes left China. Sallie was deeply depressed and missed her son, whom she had sent to the United States for school. Lottie knew Sallie had to leave for her own well-being, but they had been ministry partners for nearly a decade. Lottie couldn't imagine the long treks through villages and countryside without Sallie next to her.

"I'm going to miss you," Lottie admitted on her last afternoon with Sallie. "I don't know how I can do all this without you. You've taught me everything I know."

Sallie laughed. "You give me too much credit, Lottie Moon. I feel like I've learned as much from you as you have from me. I think you were made for China, and China was made for you. All I did was point you in the right direction."

"But it's a lot of work for one person! I'll feel so alone."

"You will never be alone," Sallie reminded her. "God will always be with you. And if you need a companion, Martha Crawford can help you. Besides, I've heard your letters have stirred up quite the missionary spirit in the South. I predict more workers will be headed to China in no time."

"I hope you're right," Lottie said, hugging Sallie. "There is always more work, it seems, than there are hands to do it."

After Sallie left, Lottie moved into Sallie's old home. It was a sprawling compound made up of three houses and a few outbuildings. Nestled in the heart of Tengchow, it was a perfect home base for outreach activities throughout the region. Lottie dubbed it "Little Crossroads," and the name stuck.

The long, low buildings of Little Crossroads were soon bustling with activity. In January 1882, two young Southern Baptist missionaries—Cicero Pruitt and N. "Weston" Halcomb—arrived in Tengchow and moved into the empty houses at Little Crossroads. During the tedious trip to China, Cicero Pruitt fell in love with a single missionary on the same ship, Miss Ida Tiffany, who was sent to China by another denominational group. Shortly after her arrival in China, Ida became a Southern Baptist, and she and Cicero were married. Ida happily joined the enthusiastic band at Little Crossroads.

With the three new missionaries and all the boarding school girls, the property was becoming quite crowded, but Lottie loved it. She welcomed the help, fresh energy, and new ideas. The young missionaries, in turn, loved and respected Lottie, who had become nearly legendary in the South for her passionate letters and tireless work in China. They peppered her with questions and drank in her words of experience.

"I feel like we need to reach further," Cicero Pruitt said as they all sat together in the twilight. "So much of the interior has yet to be reached, yet the missionaries cluster in the treaty ports like Chefoo and Tengchow."

Lottie popped up from her chair, her tiny frame alive with excitement. "You are exactly right, young man! I have long had a vision of how we could do just that."

"Tell us your vision," Ida urged.

"You are right to say the people of the treaty ports have been exposed to the gospel, but so many just outside our area have not yet heard God's word," Lottie began, her speech animated and her hands waving. "My vision is to establish a network of mission stations extending from the treaty ports hundreds of miles into the interior. Each station would be run by a missionary or team of missionaries. The outreach would be remarkable, but the network and connectivity would prevent the traditional isolation that comes with such work."

"How long have you been polishing this idea?" Cicero Pruitt asked.

"I think it began with my first village visit," Lottie admitted with a grin. "I had only been in China three weeks, but I had already seen enough to know how enormous the task was, and how much the people in the outlying areas needed the gospel. The idea has been growing ever since."

The young missionaries caught Lottie's enthusiasm. Fueled by her vision, they threw themselves into learning the language, culture, and customs in preparation for ministry in the interior. As she watched their preparations, Lottie began to sense God wanted her to be a part of the vision, not just its architect. Although her school in Tengchow was finally growing, with nearly forty students, it was simply not her mission field anymore.

Late in 1883, a contagious fever broke out in Tengchow and ran its course through Lottie's school. For their own protection and health, Lottie had to send her students home for a while. It seemed like a natural breaking point, and Lottie made the difficult decision to disband the school she had worked so hard to establish. She had enjoyed teaching and mentoring the girls, but her heart was drawn to the villages and the people beyond, hundreds of miles away from the nearest missionary. Lottie knew those were the places she ultimately needed to go.

As 1883 turned to 1884, a young female Southern Baptist missionary named Mattie Roberts arrived at Little Crossroads. Lottie liked her immediately, and so did the others who were staying there. In fact, Weston Halcomb liked her so much he married her a few months later! The Halcombs and Pruitts learned and planned eagerly together, and soon they were ready to embark on a new mission.

The two couples headed for Hwanghsien, a large city about twenty miles into the interior. Though the welcome was hesitant and the work was slow, a small church was soon established. Hwanghsien became the first station in Lottie's envisioned network. She was overjoyed, but her happiness was soon crushed by tragedy.

After just a short time in Hwanghsien, Ida Pruitt became very sick and was rushed back to Tengchow. She was treated by a missionary doctor from Chefoo and nursed by Lottie, but her body was simply too weak. She died in her husband's arms on their second anniversary. A few months later, after less than a year of marriage, Mattie Halcomb also became ill and died. It was a time of many tears at Little Crossroads.

Lottie was discouraged, and she wondered if there was any hope left for her vision. But more missionaries began to arrive, and the heartbroken husbands—Cicero Pruitt and Weston Halcomb—fought on faithfully, expanding the mission at Hwanghsien and reaching out to the surrounding villages. They soon contacted Lottie about working in the city of P'ingtu, over 100 miles into the interior of China. They had scouted out the city and found it to be an ideal location for a second mission station. They wondered if Lottie might be interested in working there.

Lottie had some trips and projects to wrap up before she could make such a long journey. In the fall of 1885, she was finally able to visit P'ingtu. It was a four-day trip from Tengchow. The days were spent bumping along uncomfortably in a shentze, and the nights were spent tossing and turning on the dirty, tick-ridden bedding of rat-infested roadside inns. But at the end of the journey, Lottie was pleasantly surprised.

P'ingtu was a large, wealthy, walled city surrounded by fertile farmlands and a scattering of small villages. The people of P'ingtu were eager to hear and learn new things, and they seemed very teachable. Near the end of her month-long visit, Lottie wrote that the people of the city were "groping ignorantly after God."

The desire and needs of the people were obvious to Lottie, but moving to P'ingtu was a big decision. She would be more than a hundred miles from her friends and the city she had come to know as her home. She would face loneliness, isolation, fear, and perhaps danger. Besides, no Southern Baptist woman had ever opened a new mission station alone. Still, she felt her heart pulling her toward P'ingtu. Did she really have the skills and strength to make her vision a reality?

The P'ingtu Project

On her own, Lottie did not have the skills and strength she needed, but she had learned over the years that with God, nothing was impossible. She returned from her month in P'ingtu with the certainty that was where God wanted her. With that certainty ringing in her heart, she quickly began packing the belongings she would need if she were to stay in P'ingtu until summer.

In a coincidence only God could orchestrate, two members of the Tengchow Baptist Church were from the city of P'ingtu. One of them, Mr. Chao, was also a servant in the Crawfords' household where Lottie and Eddie had stayed when they first came to China. Mr. Chao had travelled with Lottie on her first trip to P'ingtu, helping her find safe places to stay, showing her around the city, and teaching her the local dialect and customs. When Lottie decided to move to P'ingtu more permanently, Mr. and Mrs. Chao offered to go with her as helpers and housekeepers.

Lottie was overwhelmed with gratitude at this offer, and she quickly accepted. The Chaos finished their work for the Crawfords while Lottie finished her preparations and readied Little Crossroads for her absence. The day before her departure, Lottie took out an oversized trunk. She carefully and efficiently packed it with plenty of warm underwear, some bedding, a small rolled mattress to soften the kang she knew she would be sleeping on, an assortment of medicines, and some books. She added some foods that would not spoil easily, as she had never truly grown to enjoy most of the native Chinese foods. On top of it all, she put a small cook stove. Then she closed the trunk, which would also serve as her only piece of furniture.

In December 1885, Lottie and Mr. and Mrs. Chao set out from Tengchow in a mismatched caravan of carts, trunks, shentzes, and donkeys. They endured four cold, hard days of travel and three long, sleepless nights in the Chinese inns. When they finally reached P'ingtu, Mr. Chao contacted his cousin about a house for Lottie.

"Good news, Miss Moon," Mr. Chao announced as he returned from visiting his cousin. "I have found you a house!"

Lottie cringed inside. She knew sometimes the Chinese people looked for different features in a house than she did.

"Did you see the house, Mr. Chao?"

"Oh yes," he said with a proud grin. "It is very nice—perfect for you, Miss Moon."

"Perhaps I should go with you to see it tomorrow, before we finalize the arrangement," Lottie decided.

"Yes. That will be fine. We will go first thing in the morning."

Lottie and Mr. Chao strolled through the streets of P'ingtu the next morning, just as the city was coming to life. Merchants were laying out their wares in the marketplace, and the sunlight was just kissing the rooftops of the long, low houses. They walked past an ornate temple, and Lottie turned curiously to Mr. Chao.

"I know they worship many gods here in P'ingtu," Lottie said. "What god do they worship in this temple?"

"My people are searching so hard for the One True God that I have come to know," Mr. Chao said with sadness in his wide brown eyes. "This temple is built to 'The Unknown god'."

"Just like the people of Athens in Acts 17," Lottie mused. "These people are searching for the very same God that is waiting for them. What a harvest we might have in this city!"

When they arrived at the house, Lottie was pleasantly surprised. It was a four-room house right in the heart of the city. It was clean and in good repair, which was rare among available city houses. The first room was perfect for a kitchen, the next small room could be a storeroom, the third was a perfect passageway, and the fourth was an ideal combination bedroom, living room, and receiving room for guests. All four rooms were lined up in a row, in the traditional Chinese style.

"How much does your cousin want for this house?"

"Just $24 for the entire year," Mr. Chao answered enthusiastically. "It is a very good price."

"It is a very good price," Lottie agreed. "And this house will suit my needs very well. Please tell your cousin I will take the house."

The arrangements were made, and all the details were negotiated. Mr. and Mrs. Chao would come to help Lottie during the day and stay with relatives at night, as the little house was really only designed for one person. Lottie's things were delivered to the house, and she began to settle in. She swept the dirt floor and put a paper ceiling over the exposed rafters. She tacked paper up over the open windows and spread mats and straw rugs on the floors. Finally, she rolled out her mattress and bedding and put it on the mud brick kang. Then she stepped back, dusted off her hands, and surveyed her work.

"Home sweet home," she said with a smile.

Lottie started making connections in P'ingtu by simply being neighborly. She tested out her language skills in the new dialect by speaking with neighbors in the streets and narrow alleyways around the little house. Before long, one neighbor had offered to do Lottie's washing, and another was hired to carry Lottie's water for each day. A third neighbor became Lottie's personal seamstress. Lottie was happy to be able to provide jobs for the community, and she was thrilled to see the budding friendships that began to emerge from these partnerships.

Lottie was invited into a few homes—mostly those of Mr. Chao's relatives—but she needed to find a way to expand her reach. As a single female missionary, Lottie couldn't stand and preach on a street corner or start a church of her own. She needed a new tactic to encourage the residents of P'ingtu to connect with her.

As she mentally reviewed her options, Lottie thought about the Virginia tea cake cookies she had learned to bake as a young girl. They had always been popular with her family and friends. She wondered if they might have the same popularity with the Chinese people, drawing them in just as they had attracted Lottie's young playmates so many years ago. She decided it was at least worth a try.

The spicy-sweet cookie aroma wafted into the alley and out to the main street. Soon, a handful of people had gathered. They milled about outside Lottie's gate to discuss the unusual scent. When Lottie came through the gate with a platter of freshly-baked cookies, the people just stared.

"Have one," Lottie offered, holding the platter out to the little group. They backed away a few steps.

"It could be poison," one man commented quietly.

"We cannot trust the foreign devil woman," another muttered.

"They are called cookies," Lottie persisted. She selected a large cookie from the platter and took a big bite. "Mmmm. They are delicious."

The little group had swelled to a small crowd. There was a strange mix of curiosity and fear in their eyes.

"If she is eating them herself, they must be okay," a little boy decided. He stepped forward and took a cookie. Lottie smiled.

"It's a trick," a woman at the back of the crowd warned loudly.

All was silent as the little boy took a tiny nibble, then a larger bite. Even the birds seemed to be holding their breath. Please let him like it, Lottie prayed silently.

With a wide grin, the little boy shoved the rest of the cookie into his mouth and gulped it down. "Mmmm! They are delicious! May I please have another one?"

"Of course," Lottie said, extending the platter.

The boy took a second cookie, and the crowd surged forward to try these new treats for themselves. Within days, cookies at Lottie's house had become a neighborhood tradition. Sometimes people even brought small gifts in exchange for the cookies. While they ate, Lottie talked with her guests and learned their stories. She was finally accepted into the P'ingtu community.

To increase her acceptance, Lottie began to dress more like the Chinese. She had her seamstress make her a quilted black coat with a rich blue topcoat. Both had wide sleeves in the traditional Chinese style, and Lottie wore them over her American clothes. She found the Chinese clothing to be warm and comfortable, and she was surprised when the people showed her more respect when she dressed like them. Lottie began to realize the barriers she was unintentionally creating by clinging so tightly to her American customs and practices. She began to see that becoming more like the Chinese people was the ultimate expression of her care for them.

Word spread quickly throughout the region that Lottie loved Jesus and loved the Chinese people. She soon began receiving more invitations than she could possibly accept. Within just a few months, Lottie made 122 visits to thirty-three different places. She was even invited to visit the highest-ranking local government official in his elaborate home. Lottie was always on the go, tired but happy.

When Cicero Pruitt came from Hwanghsien to visit Lottie in the spring of 1886, he found her living like the Chinese. Her dark hair was pulled back into a Chinese-style bun, and her overcoat engulfed her little body. She was sleeping, eating, and keeping house like her Chinese neighbors, and had adopted many of their speech patterns and mannerisms. Cicero was alarmed by Lottie's Chinese lifestyle, but she assured him that everything was alright. Despite her assurances, Cicero was worried. Many of the missionaries in their area had gone insane when living so far from other Americans. Was Lottie losing her mind?

Sharing in Sha-ling

"Are you sure you're alright?" Cicero Pruitt asked, his forehead creased with concern. "It doesn't seem normal for you to dress and act like these uncivilized Chinese villagers."

Lottie bristled slightly. "Who are we to call them uncivilized? They are just differently civilized than we are. Who is to say that we are right and they are wrong? It may be just the opposite. Besides, how will they ever listen to us if we remain separate and aloof from their culture and ways?"

"I don't know, Lottie. It seems unnatural and uncomfortable. Do you believe all missionaries should live among and like the Chinese?"

"I do," Lottie answered with confidence. She took Cicero's hands in hers in a motherly way and studied his face carefully. "We need to make them our friends before we can make them our converts."

As spring melted into summer, Lottie struggled with the heat in P'ingtu, where the temperatures often soared to over 100 degrees by mid-morning. In June, she reluctantly decided she needed to get away for a while. She left P'ingtu with the promise to return in the fall, and she headed to Little Crossroads in Tengchow. She hoped to do some reading, catch up on correspondence, and—above all—rest.

Rest proved to be elusive, however, as all around the region missionaries were becoming ill, both physically and mentally. Little Crossroads became a combination hospital and retreat, and Lottie split her time between Tengchow and Hwanghsien, caring for her fellow missionaries and their families. She spent all of the summer and fall and some of the early winter nursing overwhelmed and overworked missionaries. Those she nursed—many of whom were new to China—were in awe of Lottie's strength and spirit. She soon became known as "the mother of North China," and she wore the title well.

When things were stable at Little Crossroads, Lottie finally had a chance to return to P'ingtu, where her heart longed to be. It was April 1887, and summer was coming soon, so Lottie knew her time with the people would be limited. The residents welcomed her warmly, and in the two months before the heat set in, Lottie visited over eighty homes and taught more than a dozen girls. She worked from sunup to sundown every day, using every possible minute of daylight. When night fell, Lottie collapsed on her kang, exhausted but exuberant.

Lottie went for a short break in Tengchow during the most intense heat of summer. When she arrived at Little Crossroads, she was alarmed to learn that out of the eight missionaries who had arrived in North China in the past five years, only Cicero Pruitt remained. The rest had either died or left the field because of illness or personal issues. Over the summer, Lottie wrote many letters to churches and the Foreign Mission Board, urging them to send workers to spread the gospel in China. She also pleaded for financial support to fund the Chinese missions. She especially encouraged the women of the churches to take up special offerings during the coming Christmas season.

"I wonder," Lottie wrote, "how many of us really believe that it is more blessed to give than to receive?"

When the weather grew cooler in the fall of 1887, Lottie hurried back to P'ingtu. She settled into her old routines in the little house, surrounded by the neighbors she had come to love. One morning as she was working in her garden, Lottie looked up to see two messengers with a sedan chair arriving at her gate. She rose from the soil and went to meet them.

"How can I help you?" she asked.

"We come from Dan Ho-bang in the city of Sha-ling. He has sent us here to bring you to his home."

"And why does Mr. Dan want to see me?" Lottie asked.

"On a visit to Hwanghsien, Mr. Dan heard of the 'Jesus Way'," the messenger explained. "Now he has heard that you teach this way. Mr. Dan humbly asks that you come to his home and teach him more."

"I happily accept this invitation," Lottie said in the formal Chinese way. "Please wait while I prepare a few things for the journey. I will be ready soon."

Lottie gathered a few books and teaching materials, some clothing, and a handful of other supplies. Then she climbed into the open sedan chair for the ten mile trek. By nightfall, they had arrived at the house of Dan Ho-bang in Sha-ling. Lottie was welcomed joyfully and offered a comfortable place to sleep.

The next morning, Lottie met with and taught Dan Ho-bang and his family and another family that was interested in the "Jesus Way." Within days, the number of people Lottie was teaching had exploded from a few to dozens. She was quickly becoming overwhelmed, so she called for Mrs. Crawford to come from Tengchow to help.

By the time Mrs. Crawford arrived, she found Lottie sitting on a stack of old millstones, teaching a huge crowd on the village threshing floor. The people were learning hymns and scripture, and they were becoming believers in record numbers. Within a few weeks of Lottie's arrival, twenty of the fifty families in the village had trusted in Jesus and were ready to establish a new church.

Mrs. Crawford helped get the new church up and running, but then she had to return to her duties in Tengchow. Lottie stayed on, working fourteen-hour days and frequently traveling between Sha-ling and P'ingtu. She became more "Chinese" every day as she worked closely with the people. She adopted full Chinese dress and practiced many of their local customs. With her black hair pulled tightly back and her gently-lined face kissed by the sun, Lottie was often mistaken at first glance for a Chinese woman. And that was just the way she liked it!

Finally, the summer heat drove her back to Tengchow.

"Do you have to go, Miss Moon?" a little boy asked as he munched on a cookie and watched Lottie pack her trunk on her last afternoon in P'ingtu.

"Yes, I do. The heat is too much for me. But I promise I will be back in the fall, as soon as the weather turns cooler again."

The boy nibbled his treat thoughtfully. "And will you bake more cookies when you return?"

Lottie smiled. "Of course."

Satisfied, the little boy ran off to play with his friends. Lottie chuckled and shook her head. Whenever she went away, she missed the people of P'ingtu. She was always eager for the summer to be over so she could get back to her work with them.

When Lottie arrived in Tengchow, she found she could not rest. She was too accustomed to long days of hard work. Restless and still bubbling with energy, Lottie traveled to Central China to help some missionaries establish a work among the women there. She expected it to take only a few weeks, but the project stretched far into the autumn months.

In late October, Lottie finally made it back to Little Crossroads. A few days later, as evening was falling and Lottie was just finishing a lengthy letter to the

Foreign Mission Board, she heard a voice at her gate. She immediately recognized two men from the Sha-ling church. They were dusty and worn, with tired eyes, but they brightened when they saw Lottie.

"Oh, Miss Moon," one of them said, "we are so glad to find you here!"

"Is something wrong? What brings you to Tengchow?"

The men exchanged puzzled glances. "You," one of them replied. "We walked 120 miles to find you."

Fear versus Faith

Now Lottie was puzzled. "You came all this way to look for me? Why?"

"You told us you would be back when the weather turned cooler. When you didn't come, we were worried something might have happened to you along the way. So we came to Tengchow to find you."

Lottie felt uncharacteristic tears prick her eyelids. She was deeply touched by the love and concern of the people of Sha-ling.

"I was delayed unexpectedly in Central China, sharing the 'Jesus Way,'" Lottie apologized. "But I am back now, and I will come very soon."

Within days, Lottie and Mrs. Crawford, who had promised to come and minister in the villages for a while, were on the road to P'ingtu and Sha-ling. Blustery November winds buffeted the bouncing shentzes, and both missionaries were glad when they arrived at the long, low house in P'ingtu. The residents greeted them with great fanfare and shouts of joy.

Lottie and Mrs. Crawford immediately launched into a hectic schedule of teaching and village visits. They worked faithfully through the long winter and spring. When the summer heat set in, Lottie again promised to return—much sooner this time. The people promised to continue praying and singing and worshipping together.

Soon after their return to Tengchow in the summer of 1889, Lottie and Mrs. Crawford welcomed four new missionaries. There were two single ladies—Fannie Knight and Laura Barton—and a couple, Mr. and Mrs. George Bostwick. Lottie was ecstatic. The help was desperately needed, and she was eager to train the newcomers so they could begin to minister to the people.

Lottie took on the task of training Fannie and Laura while Mrs. Crawford trained the Bostwicks. After a few weeks of training, the veteran missionaries met to discuss future assignments for their trainees.

"I believe Fannie is well suited for work in remote areas," Lottie commented. "I would like to take her to P'ingtu with me in the fall."

"Very well," said Mrs. Crawford. "I think the Bostwicks could also do well out of the city. Perhaps we could send them to help Cicero Pruitt in Hwanghsien."

"Agreed. And Laura can stay here in the city and help you. She seems ideally suited to city life."

Mrs. Crawford smiled. "Some help would be very nice."

With that, it was settled. P'ingtu and Sha-ling welcomed Lottie and Fannie in September. Lottie was pleased to find the believers in both cities growing in spirit and increasing in number. In Sha-ling, the situation was particularly noticeable, and Lottie decided the time had come to formally organize a church. She called for Cicero Pruitt and George Bostwick—both ordained ministers—to come and help with the process.

They came and baptized several members and explained the rights and responsibilities of a church. From this, the Sha-ling Baptist Church was born. It was the first Christian church of any kind in the P'ingtu region, and only the fourth Southern Baptist church in all of North China.

The church at Sha-ling was alive with enthusiasm and infused with God's Spirit. But as the church grew, so did persecution. On the day of the organization of Sha-ling Baptist Church, a young lady was baptized. After her baptism, she approached Lottie with a shy smile. Then, in a burst of impulsive joy, she threw her arms around the little lady's neck.

"How can I ever thank you aright for having come to bring me the good news of salvation?" she whispered in Lottie's ear.

Lottie smiled and gave the girl an affectionate squeeze. Later, she learned that girl was about to be married into an unbelieving household. On her wedding day, she would be required to worship her new husband's ancestors, but as a believer she planned to refuse. In Chinese culture, such a refusal could have major consequences, including torture and even death.

On the night of the girl's wedding, the Sha-ling Baptist Church gathered to pray. In the morning, the newlywed girl sent a messenger to her fellow believers.

"Good news!" the messenger proclaimed. "She has explained her beliefs to her husband and mother-in-law. After much discussion, they have agreed to allow her to keep and practice her Christian beliefs. They will not require her to worship the ancestors, and there will be no punishment."

Shouts of rejoicing rang out among the church members, and believers embraced each other in joy. Such spiritual victories were few and far between for Chinese Christians. In fact, just a few months later, another young bride from Sha-ling Baptist church was taunted, tortured, and eventually killed by her mother-in-law for practicing her Christian beliefs. As the most powerful member of the family, the mothers-in-law had control over what could happen in the household. Many were simply not willing to bend the ancient Chinese traditions.

In times of sadness, the church members looked to Lottie for direction and encouragement. She prayed that she could constantly point them toward Jesus, the Source of all hope. Even the men sought Lottie's comfort and counsel. One day, as Lottie sat in her garden, she saw an old man approaching her gate. She motioned him in and brought him some food and tea.

"What brings you here today, friend?"

The man studied his teacup self-consciously. "I have been listening when you teach the women on the threshing floor in Sha-ling. I stand just outside, where no one can see me, but I can still hear you."

Lottie smiled gently into his wide brown eyes, fringed by snowy lashes. "You are always welcome to listen."

"I want to know more about the 'Jesus Way.' I want to become His follower."

Lottie patiently explained the concept of belief in Jesus and His sacrifice on the cross. Tears streamed down the old man's leathery cheeks as he fully grasped the story and believed with all his heart. Swallowing back her own lump of emotion, Lottie prayed with the man and gave him a pocket-sized New Testament.

"Thank you," he said, bowing again and again. "I cannot read it myself, but there are those in my house who can read to me. And when they hear its truths, perhaps they too will believe."

But the old man's hopes were dashed by his sons and other family members. They locked him up and called him crazy. They threatened to take his Bible. They refused to read to him and pressured him to renounce his new-found beliefs. They said he was too old and too foolish to understand what he was doing. But the old man remained steadfast in his faith—which utterly frustrated his sons.

Finally it was agreed that Li Show-ting, a close relative, would read the New Testament to the stubborn man. Li Show-ting was a scholar of Confucianism, a religion centered on the human wisdom of Confucius.

He looked forward to reading the Bible and pointing out all the flaws and inconsistencies he expected to find. To his surprise and the old man's delight, the message he read was far from flawed. It made sense and impacted his soul in a remarkable way.

Li Show-ting came to Lottie's house one afternoon with a heart full of hope and a head full of questions. Lottie taught him what she could, but many of his questions were intellectual and deeply theological. Frustrated by her lack of training in theology, Lottie called for other missionaries to help. After several days of intense investigation, Li Show-ting chose to become a believer, and he was accepted into the church at Sha-ling.

The old man's faithful witness had helped draw Li Show-ting to the truth. What no one knew at that time was that Li Show-ting would go on to become the greatest evangelist North China had ever seen. History reports more than 10,000 Chinese believed in Jesus and were baptized under Pastor Li's ministry.

For a short time, the persecution seemed to wane, but the Chinese New Year in early 1890 brought fresh trouble. Because ancestor worship played such a large role in Chinese New Year festivities, it became suddenly obvious to everyone that Christians were no longer participating in ancestor worship. As this realization dawned through the community, it sparked anger and violence. Ancestor worship was required to bring New Year's blessings on families and communities.

Friends, relatives, and neighbors of the Christians were desperate to make them renounce their faith and participate in the pagan worship.

Li Show-ting was badly beaten for refusing to worship the ancestors. He was dragged through the city by his hair and left, bleeding and bruised, with part of his scalp torn from his head. Weakened and fearful, he fled Sha-ling for the safety of P'ingtu, where he was not known. Despite the brutal torture, Li Show-ting clung to his faith and refused to recant.

As Lottie listened to the shouting throughout the city of P'ingtu, she prayed for the believers who were facing persecution. At that moment, a breathless voice shouted at her gate.

"Miss Moon! Miss Moon! I have run all the way from Sha-ling. You must come. Now!"

Lottie was already grabbing her overcoat. "What is it? What has happened?"

"They beat Li Show-ting and drove him from the city. Now they have pulled old Dan Ho-bang from his home. They shouted at him and kicked him and spat on him. Then they tied his hands and feet to a pole and started beating him. Still, he refuses to renounce his faith."

Lottie called for a sedan chair, and she urged the chair-bearers to run as much as possible along the wide road to Sha-ling. With a heavy heart, she prayed she would not be too late.

When she reached the city, Lottie went directly to the town square. There was Dan Ho-bang, crumpled on the ground, still tied to a pole. His eyes were nearly swollen shut, puffy and blackened, and there was dried blood crusted on his face and clothing. Fresh blood oozed from a split and disfigured lip. An unruly mob shouted insults at him and kicked his stomach. Small boys threw stones at him. Lottie felt anger rise in her throat.

Drawing herself up to her full 4-foot 3-inches, Lottie elbowed through the crowd. She knelt over the battered body of Dan Ho-bang.

"I am here, Mr. Dan," she whispered.

The old man's face brightened as he recognized her voice. He tried to smile.

"Oh, Miss Moon—I knew you would come."

Lottie turned to face the mob, which had grown strangely quiet. Her dark eyes flashed fiercely, and her voice rang out across the open square.

"If you attempt to destroy this church, you will have to kill me first. Jesus gave Himself for us Christians. Now, I am ready to die for Him."

Surprised glances raced across the faces of the crowd. They had not expected such courage from the little foreign lady. Most turned and drifted away, but a few hovered menacingly around Dan Ho-bang. One man waved his long knife at Lottie.

"I will kill you, foreign devil," he promised in a low growl.

The Show-ting believers trickled into the square and helped move Mr. Dan to the safety of a house. Then a young lady from the church grabbed Lottie's arm and waved fearfully toward the man with the knife, still lingering near the house.

"That man is evil, Miss Moon. He really will kill you. You should go home to P'ingtu."

Lottie shook her head firmly. "Only believe, dear one. Do not fear. Our Master, Jesus, always watches over us, and no matter what the persecution, Jesus will surely overcome it."

When Dan Ho-bang was well enough to travel, Lottie took him with her to P'ingtu, where Li Show-ting was already staying. The two men recovered quickly under Lottie's careful care. While in P'ingtu, Mr. Dan and Mr. Li helped establish the first seeds of a church in the city. When they were well enough, they also conducted outreach to nearby villages. Believers throughout the region were encouraged, and the persecution had a beneficial effect. Instead of damaging and destroying the church, the tribulations made the believers in P'ingtu and Sha-ling some of the strongest in all of China.

The persecution also drove Lottie and Fannie—who were working together in P'ingtu that winter—closer together. Lottie loved Fannie's enthusiasm and found her a fast and eager learner. Fannie, in turn, adored and admired Lottie. Fannie wrote about Lottie to her family, saying, "I think I might safely say that no missionary is making greater sacrifices than she." As she watched Fannie face the persecution fearlessly,

Lottie knew she had finally found someone who could manage the ministry in P'ingtu. With a flood of relief and thankfulness, Lottie made preparations for a much needed furlough. But she wondered if her heart would ever find peace anywhere but China.

Christianity in Crisis

Lottie sailed from Shanghai in the summer of 1891. It was a calm voyage, but Lottie—never much good on boats—was plagued with headaches and seasickness. She landed at San Francisco and took a train to the familiar rolling hills of Virginia. It was good to be home, but it also felt strange. Virginia felt almost as foreign to her as China once had. In many ways, the United States simply wasn't home to Lottie anymore.

Viewmont had been sold off to strangers, and the bulk of the money was used to pay debts. What was left was divided equally among the surviving siblings. Eddie took her portion and Lottie's portion and purchased a small home for them to share. It was nestled in a grove of trees, just a few miles down the road from Viewmont, near the town of Scottsville. Eddie named the little cottage and surrounding property Bonheur.

Bonheur was a lovely place for Lottie to rest and recuperate. She had her own room with a big soft bed piled high with pillows. The floors were covered with thick, luxurious rugs, and a marble-topped dresser stood in the corner. Along one wall was a beautiful fireplace. Another wall had wide windows that overlooked a small orchard. A cow named Belle grazed in the little pasture, and a handful of chickens scratched in the dirt that ringed the little house.

Lottie spent her first six months of furlough at Bonheur. She took long walks through the forests and fields of her childhood romps. She read books and slept as much as she wanted. She visited with family and old friends, and she simply basked in an overwhelming sense of peace.

But the peace Lottie felt at Bonheur was in stark contrast to the turmoil that was brewing among the missionaries back in China. T.P. Crawford was waging his own private war against the Foreign Mission Board, insisting it was corrupt and poorly structured. He decided to break away and start his own mission organization, unconnected to the Southern Baptists. With his forceful personality and persistent nature, Crawford drew away many of the North China missionaries, including—eventually—even Lottie's own dear Fannie Knight who was ministering in P'ingtu. Unkind and unchristian remarks flew across the continents, and the ministry to the Chinese was both neglected and damaged as a result.

Lottie spoke often with H.A. Tupper, head of the Foreign Mission Board, about the situation in China. She also talked with Cicero Pruitt, who was on furlough and fully understood the problems the dispute was creating. Lottie felt heartbroken and helpless, so many thousands of miles away from where she wanted and needed to be. She was frustrated with her fellow missionaries, and her heart ached for the Chinese believers who could be led astray or disillusioned by such infighting. She prayed each day that the believers would not be distracted by the division among the foreigners.

In spite of her desire to be in China, Lottie patiently made her way from church to church, speaking in ladies' meetings, attending dinner parties, making appearances at conventions, and answering hundreds of questions about the land that held her heart. She spoke about life in China—the good and bad aspects. She told about faith and persecution, about hope and hardships. She argued vehemently against the idea the Chinese were uncivilized, insisting that a different culture was not the same as a lack of culture. She explained the Chinese people were bright, kind, talented individuals who learned and lived and loved in the same ways Lottie's American listeners did.

As part of her travels, Lottie attended the 1892 Southern Baptist Convention in Atlanta, Georgia. At the convention, a giant crimson silk banner was displayed. It was a gift from the believers at Sha-ling. Along with the banner, the Chinese Christians had sent a note that said, "We thank God that He gave His servants wisdom to choose and send so good a missionary as Miss Moon, whose heart is filled with love like that unto the Son of God." Lottie was deeply touched and humbled by these words, but they also made her desperately homesick for China and the Chinese people.

Churches all over the South pleaded for Lottie to visit and speak to them. She had more invitations than she could possibly accept, but she did her best to visit as many places as possible. Whenever Lottie spoke, people were moved. They gave money. They surrendered their lives to mission work. They became faithful in prayer support. God used Lottie to change hearts and transform lives throughout her furlough. People were astounded by her strength, encouraged by her spirit, and inspired by her love for the work in China. At one engagement, Lottie was questioned about the trials of missionary life.

"People talk of the hardships of missionary life," Lottie answered, her head tilted thoughtfully. "'Tis true there are hardships. But I am so happy in the work that I never mind them."

That happiness was fully realized when Lottie sailed back to China in November 1893. She was feeling less and less attached to the United States, and she had been away from her beloved China for more than two years. Much had changed while she was gone. The Crawfords had left Tengchow as part of the missionary conflict, and many of the other missionaries had also left the Shantung Province region. Mrs. Crawford sent Lottie a lengthy, tear-stained letter asking her to continue to guide the Tengchow women Mrs. Crawford had invested much of her life in discipling.

With so many changes, Lottie had a great deal of work to do in Tengchow. There were multiple schools to manage and village ministries to continue. After much prayer, Lottie decided to make Little Crossroads in Tengchow her permanent home base and focus her energies on the city and surrounding villages. There were a handful of younger missionaries who had arrived during Lottie's absence, and they were happily involved with the ministries at P'ingtu, Sha-ling, and Hwanghsien.

Lottie still felt deeply connected to the believers in that region, however, so in May 1894, she made a two-month trip to P'ingtu and Sha-ling to visit her dear friends there. Just before she left on furlough, Lottie had purchased a small piece of land in Sha-ling and donated it to the believers there. When she visited, the church members proudly showed Lottie the Chinese-style church and school they had built on the land. Over forty new believers had joined the church as well, making Sha-ling Baptist Church the largest Southern Baptist congregation in North China.

The believers in P'ingtu also welcomed Lottie with open arms. They had grown in number and strengthened in spirit, and they were following Lottie's example in reaching out to the surrounding villages with the gospel. Lottie spent time teaching, encouraging, and fellowshipping with all the believers before heading back to Tengchow. And she made her friends promise to check in with her anytime they visited her city.

Back in Tengchow, Lottie dived into village work.

There were over 100 villages within a day's journey of the city, and between August and October 1894, Lottie visited 84 of them. She made connections with the believers in each village and reached out to those who did not yet believe. She taught hymns and scripture, refreshed the teachings Mrs. Crawford had instilled, and told Bible stories to the women and girls. Many men loitered nearby so they, too, could hear the message about the "Jesus Way." Lottie's typical day ran from dawn to dusk with only a brief stop for lunch each day. She was virtually tireless!

As the village ministries developed and grew, so did the political problems in China. In late 1894, China and Japan went to war, and foreigners were immediately tagged as spies for Japan. The hostility toward all foreigners—including missionaries—was worse in treaty ports like Tengchow, so Lottie decided to spend the Christmas season inland in P'ingtu. She had a wonderful time and didn't head back to Tengchow until mid-January.

Just past Hwanghsien on the road to Tengchow, Lottie noticed an unusual number of people on the roads. It was a cold, gray day, but the people slogged through the icy slush with sad faces and purposeful strides. As they drew closer to Tengchow, Lottie saw women with crying babies and small children struggling along. Old men and women, bent with age and illness, pushed through the muck with heavy bundles on their backs. Silent tears ran down weathered cheeks.

"What is happening?" Lottie asked an old woman as she passed. "Where is everyone going?"

The old woman looked at Lottie, her eyes hollow pools of fear and exhaustion. "The Japanese have bombed Tengchow. Everything is destroyed. We do not know where we are going. We are just going away."

With a seed of fear growing in the pit of her stomach, Lottie and her chair-bearers pressed on against the tide of refugees. When they reached Tengchow, Lottie found Little Crossroads damaged, but livable. A bomb had obliterated much of the porch and blown a hole in the wall of the main house, but Lottie could work around that. She quickly learned the other missionaries and foreigners had fled to Chefoo, but Lottie had missed the boat. She considered going back to P'ingtu, but no one was available to take her. As she weighed her options, a local government official arrived at her gate.

"Ah, Miss Moon, I am glad to find you here."

He bowed deeply, and Lottie returned the bow. "How may I be of service to you?" she asked.

"I understand your fellow missionaries have gone on to Chefoo without you. Will you be staying here in Tengchow?"

"I have not yet decided," Lottie answered.

The official tried to look very important and stern. "I would like to ask you to stay here in the city. Your presence has a calming effect on our people, it seems."

Lottie thought for a moment. "Can you assure my safety?"

"Well...no," the official admitted. "But both sides have agreed to respect the safety of anyone flying the American flag. That would help."

Lottie ended up staying in Tengchow throughout the conflict, and the people greatly respected her for it. Her travel and ministry were limited during that time, but when the war was over, people flocked to the church in Tengchow and begged Lottie to come to their villages. At fifty-six years old, Lottie was getting tired, but she was determined to press on. She managed all her ministries in the city and aimed to visit two villages each day——one in the morning, followed by a short lunch break, and another village in the afternoon.

After a lunch break at a believer's house in one of the villages, Lottie was exhausted. She asked to rest on the kang for a short while before going on to the next village, and the hostess was happy to oblige. When Lottie awoke, she hurried to her next stop, running late. She hoped her tardiness would not be noticed, but she was dismayed to find a large crowd waiting patiently for her.

The people crushed around Lottie as she climbed onto a kang to sit and teach. Small girls filled the floor in front of her, and old women climbed up beside her on the kang so they could hear. Middle-aged women stood in the back of the room, and men loitered outside the paper-covered windows. Lottie explained the "Jesus Way" and told the crowd about the promise of Heaven.

One woman near the back of the room spoke up, saying, "But Heaven is for people like you, Miss Moon. Heaven could never be for people like us."

Around the room, heads bobbed in agreement. Lottie's heart squeezed with compassion.

"Oh no," Lottie told them, meeting the hungry eyes one by one. "Heaven is most certainly for you. Heaven is for everyone who believes in the 'Jesus Way.' That is why I have come."

1896 and 1897 were hectic, difficult years for Lottie. They were plagued with sickness, death, crime, and challenges for the Southern Baptist missionaries in North China. Lottie's days were a whirlwind of teaching school, leading Sunday school, conducting men's Bible classes, nursing ailing missionaries, and visiting villages regularly. There were long, hard days when Lottie was sure things couldn't possibly get any worse. But the persecution and problems were about to explode.

Running from the Rebellion

For several years, Lottie had suspected the Empress Dowager of China and other key government officials were actively encouraging anti-Christian and anti-foreign feelings and actions. In 1900, Lottie's suspicions were confirmed when the government became more open in their hostile attitudes. Because she worked so closely with the people, Lottie often heard tidbits of gossip and insider information. When she heard on good authority that the Empress Dowager's government was secretly offering support to the Boxers, Lottie reported it to John Fowler, the U.S. Consul at Chefoo.

The Boxers were a group of murderous insurgents who were terrorizing China. They roamed the roads creating mayhem and fear. They robbed travelers, beat those that resisted them, and vandalized and looted businesses. And they seemed to have a particular hatred of foreigners and Christians, targeting them with special brutality. It was almost unthinkable that the government would support such a group, but the anti-foreign and anti-Christian sentiments were growing in popularity at both the national and local levels.

These negative attitudes were demonstrated openly when a local government magistrate who ruled over the cities of P'ingtu and Laichow falsely accused thirteen Christians of robbery. He had the men arrested and ordered soldiers to tie the men's traditional long pigtails to the saddle horns of the fastest cavalry horses. Then he ordered the horses to be driven at a gallop all the way to the next town, several miles away. The accused Christians tried to run alongside the horses, but as they became tired or stumbled, their bodies were dragged by their hair over the bumpy, rocky roads. Bleeding, bruised, and battered, they were thrown into the jail at P'ingtu.

As they often did in times of desperation, the P'ingtu believers turned to Lottie Moon. They sent a messenger to Tengchow, begging for help. Lottie listened with mounting indignation as the messenger told her everything that had happened.

"Will you come, Miss Moon?"

Lottie thought for a moment. The roads were very dangerous with bands of Boxers on the loose. A foreign female missionary was a prime target for these marauders. She knew her Tengchow friends would warn her not to go. But how could she desert the people in their time of need? How could she tell them God was always listening and always ready to come to their aid if she herself was not? She knew this was an ideal opportunity to demonstrate God's love and power to the people of P'ingtu. Suddenly she had an idea.

"Of course I will come," Lottie gently assured the messenger. "I have a plan, but we must work quickly.

Do you think you can find someone who will lend you a government shentze? I need the large kind with a crossbar and heavy curtains."

The messenger nodded eagerly. "I think I can do that."

"Excellent," Lottie said. "Have the shentze here in an hour. I will be ready."

The messenger hurried off, and Lottie sent word to a government friend. Soon a porter arrived at her gate with a bundle of clothing. She paid the porter and began her preparations. Lottie unwound her long, straight black hair from the careful bun she always wore. She combed it straight back and into a low ponytail at the nape of her neck, just like the Chinese men did. Then she dressed in the clothes the porter had brought: a long black Chinese man's robe and slacks and the short red overcoat traditionally worn by government officials. To finish the disguise, Lottie donned wide-rimmed black glasses and a small black cap with the official red button on top. She surveyed herself in a small mirror. Everything was perfect!

Right on time, the messenger returned with an ornate shentze borrowed from another official who was happy to do a favor for the popular Miss Moon. When the messenger arrived at the gate and Lottie stepped out, he hesitated.

"I'm sorry, sir," he murmured, bowing deeply. "I was looking for Miss Moon."

Lottie's well-practiced condescending frown melted into a silly grin. "It's me," she whispered, giggling at the messenger's surprise. "Now, let's get going."

Lottie climbed into the shentze and the messenger ran alongside. All the way to P'ingtu—for four grueling days of travel—Lottie wore her costume and sat at the mouth of the shentze. The heavy curtains were parted, and Lottie sat ramrod straight, a permanent frown creasing her stern face. Her back ached and her eyes watered, but she kept up the ruse, determined to stick to her plan. All along the route, people waved and bowed in respect, assuming she was an important official, and the Boxers scattered as she came into view. Still, Lottie breathed a sigh of relief when the journey was finally at an end.

In P'ingtu, Lottie learned the thirteen men had been released, but they had also been terribly tortured. She agreed to stay in P'ingtu for a while to nurse the injured Christians back to health. Within the tight-knit group of believers, the messenger told and re-told the story of his journey with Lottie Moon. The P'ingtu Christians laughed out loud every time they heard the tale of little Lottie's elaborate plan. Her courage and dedication to them made them love her even more.

Soon the vagabond groups of roaming Boxers had organized themselves into the Boxer Rebellion. The crackdown on foreigners and Christians became increasingly intense. Lottie's mere presence in the city of P'ingtu put the believers there at risk. Throughout the region, missionary homes, schools, and churches were being looted and destroyed. Believers were safest when they distanced themselves from the foreign missionaries.

In response to the violence and destruction, Lottie and the other Southern Baptist missionaries retreated to Tengchow at the urging of the Chinese believers. At first it seemed like a safe enough option, but the Boxer Rebellion became even more brutal and widespread. U.S. Consul John Fowler finally ordered all Americans out of Shantung Province on July 1, 1900. The missionaries fled to a makeshift refugee camp in Chefoo.

There was nothing to do at the camp, no outreach or ministry to undertake, no way to learn or grow. Lottie quickly grew intolerably bored. On a whim, she booked passage to Shanghai, and then on to Fukuoka, Japan. Lottie considered herself incapable of sitting idle while a political conflict dragged on indefinitely. If she could not minister in her beloved China, she decided she would join the mission work in Japan until she was able to go home to Shantung Province.

Lottie was in Japan from late July 1900 until April 1901. During those nine months, Lottie taught at an English commercial school. The school allowed teachers to choose their own textbooks for English classes. Characteristically, Lottie chose the Bible for her classes. As she taught English, she also taught the way of salvation, and the response was remarkable. Through her teaching, three Japanese young men came to know Jesus, and many other lives were impacted forever. When the trouble was over and Lottie was able to head back to China, her students promised to write to her, and she promised to stop in Japan on her next furlough.

In April 1901, Lottie sailed for China again. She knew the political landscape of the country had changed, and she had heard stories of believers who were tortured and even killed by the Boxers. She knew the hearts and commitment of the Chinese Christians in Shantung Province, but such opposition could sway even the most dedicated believer. Deep in her soul, Lottie was fearful about what she might find on her return.

The Relief of Return

There were few Boxer uprisings after Lottie's return to China, but the nation had been forever changed. The Boxer Rebellion had resulted in the deaths of more than 32,000 Chinese and 230 foreign missionaries. Such loss was staggering. Some of the church members had been martyred, killed for their refusal to reject their faith, but Lottie rejoiced to find the core of the Chinese church had survived. The stories of the martyrs and the enduring faithfulness of the Christians inspired unbelievers to seek God in record numbers. Thousands flooded the churches, and baptisms increased exponentially over the next months and years.

As this revival was underway, new missionaries from a new generation were arriving in China. Many had grown up in Southern Baptist churches during an era in which "Lottie Moon" was a household name. They were amazed and a little bit in awe of the little legend that stood before them when they arrived. But Lottie's bright spirits and obvious love for China put them immediately at ease. This new team was eager to change the world that lay before them.

Lottie was especially excited about the incoming medical missionaries. A pretty, eager young nurse named Jessie Pettigrew came first, followed quickly by T.W. Ayers—a journalist-turned-doctor—and his family. With Lottie's help and a promised endowment from the Foreign Mission Board, they planned to establish a hospital in Hwanghsien.

Amidst all the growth and change, Lottie's schools were growing, enrolling more students each year. The prayer meetings and Bible classes she led were also well-established. When Lottie walked down the street, friends and strangers alike called out to her. She was well-known, loved, and respected in Tengchow, P'ingtu, Sha-ling, and the surrounding villages.

Although she was hesitant to leave such glorious progress, Lottie knew it was time for her to take another furlough. It had been nearly a decade since she had given in-person reports to her churches. She had also received word that both Ike and Eddie were in poor health, and Lottie's heart longed to see them one more time. With her soul torn between two desires, Lottie sailed for the United States in late 1902, stopping in Japan to visit her old students and celebrate the dawning of 1903.

When Lottie arrived in the United States, she was regarded as a bit of an oddity, like a dramatic character from a forgotten era. Her long black skirt and cape and her high-necked blouse were outdated. Her dark hair was fading to a dull gray. A few of her teeth were missing, and she had grown quite plump. But her awkward appearance was forgotten as soon as she began to speak. Lottie's sparkling conversational skills and vivacious spirit were still very much intact, and her passion bubbled through every interaction.

First, Lottie traveled to see her brother Ike and Maggie, who were both ill. They welcomed Lottie and spent many happy hours reminiscing together. Soon Eddie joined them. She, too, was ailing, and she had sold the home at Bonheur so she could use the money traveling and looking for a cure. Lottie also spent time with various nieces and nephews and other family members. It was a golden, happy time of togetherness.

As Lottie began visiting churches, she encountered many friends and acquaintances who urged her to retire. Whenever retirement was mentioned, Lottie would shake her head and laugh gently.

"Oh, don't say you don't want me to return," Lottie told one friend. "Nothing could make me stay. China is my joy and delight. It is my home now."

Lottie spent several months of her furlough traveling and speaking extensively. She was regarded as a living legend, and everyone wanted to meet her. As she spoke, Lottie always asked for help in China, and she always encouraged believers to find their personal mission field—wherever it might be—and serve there wholeheartedly.

On February 15, 1904, Lottie said goodbye to Ike and Eddie and the rest of the family. She recognized that it would likely be their last time to be all together, and the goodbyes were especially poignant. But Lottie had no doubt where she belonged. On February 27th, she boarded a boat in San Francisco and sailed for China once again.

Lottie settled back into Little Crossroads, donned the familiar Chinese clothes, and looked around. The well-worn upholstered furniture, the creaky rocking chairs, the wooden writing desk and bookcase, Eddie's old organ, the shelves and footstool and candlesticks—all added up to a true sense of home. She was grateful to be back. New doors were opening and new opportunities were on the horizon, and Lottie wanted to be a part of it all.

China was changing, clawing its way into the twentieth century. Women were being freed from bound feet and limited lives. Education was thriving, including adoption of Western ideas and the education of women. And these changes were shaping and fueling mission endeavors throughout China. Theological schools were built for men, and training colleges were established for women. The new Southern Baptist hospital was finally up and running in Hwanghsien. And everyone looked to Lottie for wisdom and guidance though the changes.

In addition to advising her fellow missionaries, Lottie oversaw several schools in Tengchow for both children and adults. She was a taskmaster, but her students loved and respected her. Lottie's students were expected to attend class six days a week and go to Sunday school and church services together on Sunday.

Lottie again opened her home up as a boarding house for more than a dozen women and girls whom she encouraged, discipled, and deeply loved.

As political problems in the region grew worse, prices went up and wages went down. Many old women and young girls—the least valued members of Chinese society—found themselves on the streets. When Lottie saw them, she welcomed them into the already-crowded quarters at Little Crossroads. She fed and cared for everyone on her own meager salary. The more mouths there were to feed, the thinner the soup became, but Lottie never turned away a person in need. Many Chinese were won to Christ simply by observing Lottie's love.

Over the next several years, Lottie traveled a little less and rested a little more, but her overall pace didn't slow much at all. She trained new missionaries and spent most of her days in the many schools she oversaw. She still made occasional visits to the villages, although they happened less frequently than before. But everywhere she went, Lottie listened. She listened to the stories of people in need. She listened to the testimonies of new believers. She listened to news around town, gossip whispered in alleyways, and the silent comments of eyes and gestures. Soon, Lottie began to sense that something was wrong, and she was right—the Boxers were back and worse than ever!

Battlefield Bravery

Fortunately, the renewed Boxer Rebellion did not sweep as far into North China as Lottie had feared. There were brief explosions of violence, but most of them were far from Shantung Province. When the danger had passed and the Rebellion had been tamped out, Lottie breathed a prayer of relief and thankfulness. There was much work to do, and she was eager to get started.

It was another era of growth and change for Chinese missions. T.P. Crawford had died, and with him went most of the energy that had propelled his independent mission group. Many of the missionaries that had originally followed Crawford found themselves wanting to work with the Southern Baptist Foreign Mission Board again, and they looked to Lottie to help negotiate their return. Through the entire ordeal, only Lottie had managed to remain good friends with people on both sides of the conflict. She was happy to mend the broken relationships, and with newfound unity, the mission team in North China was poised for great things.

This reunification also brought Martha Crawford back into Lottie's life. With her husband gone,

Mrs. Crawford was free to return to Tengchow, the city she loved. At age seventy-seven, she moved a little slower than before, but she and Lottie—now in her mid-sixties—both still had a deep desire to do village work. They held a series of evangelistic meetings in the small villages around Tengchow, and the people responded enthusiastically.

One day, Mrs. Crawford crossed town to visit Little Crossroads. Lottie welcomed her and made some tea. Then they sat together on the weathered porch.

"You will never guess who is coming to North China," Mrs. Crawford teased.

"It must be someone important to bring you all the way to my house."

Mrs. Crawford smiled knowingly. "R. J. Willingham!"

Lottie was surprised. "The head of the Foreign Mission Board is coming to China? That's a first. No member of the Board has ever visited China."

"Well, he'll be here later this year. And we are planning a great big meeting to host him right here in Tengchow!"

Extravagant preparations were made for the visit of such an important guest. But just weeks before R. J. Willingham was due to arrive, there was an outbreak of meningitis in the Tengchow schools. For the health and wellbeing of everyone, the meeting was moved to Hwanghsien. Lottie and Mrs. Crawford made the day-long journey to join in the festivities and enjoy the meetings and fellowship.

It was a glorious time, but it marked the beginning of new challenges for Lottie. Shortly after the meningitis outbreak cleared, bubonic plague broke out in Tengchow. It persisted through the late fall and Christmas season of 1907, and to prevent the spread of infection, strict curfews were imposed. Lottie was housebound and lonely. She longed for more help and companionship in the city. There had been a recent influx of new missionaries, but most had gone to the interior cities, where work seemed more productive.

In the summer of 1908, a smallpox scare had Lottie quarantined again after she cared for an infected missionary. This left her feeling even more housebound and even more alone. She was becoming frustrated at the constant parade of sickness and isolation. In the fall, when she was finally released from quarantine, Lottie was happy to undertake the mammoth task of reopening all the Tengchow schools by herself. Keeping busy distracted Lottie from the sadness that sometimes hovered over her.

Finally, in late 1908, help began to arrive in Tengchow. Several new missionaries arrived in the city, and Lottie was responsible for training many of them. Little Crossroads was bustling with activity again, and Lottie couldn't have been happier.

On January 11, 1909, Lottie received a letter from her nephew. Her hands trembled as she carefully opened the envelope. In her heart she knew what the letter would say, because it had been several weeks since she had received a letter from Eddie, who had faithfully written once a week for decades. As Lottie read the details of Eddie's death in the letter, her throat ached and tears spilled down her cheeks. She felt utterly alone in the world.

Although she was heartbroken over the loss of Eddie, Lottie swallowed her sorrow and focused on the ministry. What a change there had been since the early days of Lottie's time in China! By mid-1909, North China boasted sixteen churches with over 2000 members and fifty-six schools with over a thousand students. And Lottie was personally involved in many of those works, overseeing several missionaries and working regularly in eighteen villages, even though she was nearly seventy years old.

In 1911, revolution broke out in China with the overthrow of the old Manchu Dynasty. As the fighting arose, the plague returned, followed by severe famine. Times were hard in China. To compound the situation, the rainy season brought massive flooding that destroyed crops and drove people from their homes. Desperation and hopelessness ran rampant.

By January 1912, the fighting was intense and widespread. The U.S. Consul recommended the evacuation of all foreigners in Shantung Province. The entire mission corps from Hwanghsien fled to Chefoo, leaving the new hospital staffed only by unskilled, untrained, local laborers. Lottie was about to leave Tengchow when she heard about the evacuation of

Hwanghsien. She finished her light packing and climbed into her sedan chair.

"We have had a change in plans," she told her chair-bearers. "We will not be going to Chefoo. We will be going to Hwanghsien."

"But Miss Moon, there is much fighting on the road to Hwanghsien," one of the chair-bearers said. "Shouldn't you go to Chefoo with the other foreigners?"

Lottie shook her head stubbornly. "No. I am needed in Hwanghsien, so that is where I will go. Can you take me by some lesser-known route to get me there safely?"

The chair-bearers exchanged glances. They had carried Miss Moon many times and had learned it did no good to argue with the little lady. She always got her way in the end.

"As you wish," said the chair-bearer as he and his friend lifted the chair and started down the road.

When they reached the hospital in Hwanghsien, Lottie took command of the chaos. For ten days, she supervised and ran the entire hospital single-handedly. When the other missionaries gathered their courage and returned in spite of the continued fighting, they were shocked to find Lottie in charge. Everyone had assumed she was in Chefoo with the other missionaries.

As soon as the doctors and nurses had returned, Lottie began to pack her things.

"Where are you going?" Dr. Ayers asked.

"Home to Tengchow."

"Miss Moon," Dr. Ayers said gently, "it simply isn't safe. There is much fighting between here and there. You're likely to be shot."

"I'm sure I'll be fine," Lottie insisted.

Exasperated by her stubbornness, the missionaries sent word to contacts on both sides of the battle. The message said that Lottie Moon would be passing through the battlefield at a precise time the following morning. As Lottie and her escort entered the battlefield, the generals on both sides laid down their arms. As soon as she was gone, the vicious fighting recommenced.

"See, young man?" Lottie told the young missionary escort. "I knew I had nothing to worry about."

Lottie had the deep love and respect of people on both sides of the conflict. Her words and actions had impacted people of all walks of life. Lottie's life had truly touched all of North China and beyond.

A Lasting Legacy

Despite her influence and impact, a deep sadness was overtaking Lottie's life. She was concerned about the finances of the Foreign Mission Board, which was in significant debt. She was frustrated by the apathy of American Christians and their reluctance to give their money and lives for mission work. She was also deeply moved by the famine and sickness among the people she loved. The compound at Little Crossroads was packed full of needy, hungry, hopeless people. Lottie wanted to reach them all—she wanted to save them all.

By the time anyone realized something was wrong with Lottie, it was too late. She had stopped eating weeks before, choosing to give her food away so others could eat. The plump, round body had grown thin and frail, well-disguised by the bulky Chinese clothing she always wore. Her body was weak and sickly, and her mind was overwhelmed by worry and despair.

As news of Lottie's condition spread, missionaries came from all over North China to care for Lottie, just as she had cared for many of them. When they could do nothing more for her at home, they took her to the hospital in Hwanghsien, but even the best hospital care proved inadequate. Finally, the decision was made to send her home to the United States for care, even though the doctors doubted she was strong enough to make the journey.

Lottie was taken by shentze to the coast, where she and a nurse were booked passage on the *Manchuria*. In December 1912, when Lottie was carried on board the ship, she weighed only fifty pounds and could barely speak. She rested fitfully for the first leg of her journey, but her body was just too weak to endure the stresses of travel. In the port of Kobe, Japan—one of her favorite places—Lottie Moon went to be with Jesus on Christmas Eve, 1912.

When word of Lottie's death was announced, letters poured in to the Foreign Mission Board from all around the world. Lottie's life and example had touched the lives of thousands, and the impact of her words and actions changed the course of missions—in China and beyond. Memorials were held throughout the United States and in several other countries honoring the courage, wisdom, and faithfulness of Lottie Moon.

The people of Tengchow, where Lottie's heart had always resided, erected a monument to Lottie Moon, who had given so much of herself to them. The inscription simply read:

The Tengchow church remembers forever.

But perhaps the most enduring monument to Lottie's life and work is the annual Lottie Moon Christmas Offering taken up in Southern Baptist churches each December. Instituted in 1918, and based on Lottie's encouragement of missions giving, this offering is used to fund mission work around the globe. In many ways, this offering—Lottie's offering—is still making a difference and changing the world for Christ. Lottie's legacy lives on!

Bibliography

Allen, Catherine B. *The New Lottie Moon Story.* Nashville: Broadman Press, 1980.

Benge, Geoff and Janet. *Lottie Moon: Giving Her All for China.* Seattle: YWAM Publishing, 2001.

Jackson, Dave and Neta. *Drawn by a China Moon: Lottie Moon.* Ada, Michigan: Bethany House, 2000.

Monsell, Helen A. *Her Own Way: The Story of Lottie Moon.* Nashville: Broadman Press, 1958.

Lottie Moon Timeline

1840 Charlotte Digges "Lottie" Moon is born in Albemarle County, Virginia.

1854 Lottie attends and graduates from the Virginia Female Seminary.

1857 Lottie goes to the Albemarle Female Institute.

1858 Lottie decides to give her life to Jesus.

1860 Abraham Lincoln is elected President of the United States of America.

1861 The Civil War begins when the Confederates fire on Fort Sumter.

1861 Lottie graduates with a Master of Arts degree and is declared "the most educated woman in the South".

1865 The Civil War ends when General Robert E. Lee surrenders to General Ulysses S. Grant at the Appomattox Courthouse.

1865 Lottie begins teaching at the Danville Female Academy in Kentucky.

1871 Lottie and her friend Anna open the Cartersville Female High School in Cartersville, Georgia.

1872 Edmonia "Eddie" Moon arrives in Tengchow, China as a missionary.

1873 Lottie arrives in China as a missionary.

1876 Alexander Graham Bell invents the telephone.

1876 Lottie takes a furlough to the United States, accompanying Eddie home to Virginia and returning to China in November 1877.

1878 Lottie opens her first girls' school in China.

1884 First mission station is established at Hwanghsien.

1885	Lottie moves to P'ingtu to establish the second mission station.
1887	Dan Ho-bang sends messengers to bring Lottie to Sha-ling.
1889	Sha-ling Baptist Church is officially organized.
1891	Lottie takes her second furlough to the United States, returning to China in November 1893.
1895	Japan bombs Tengchow as part of the war with China, and Little Crossroads is damaged.
1896	Henry Ford builds the world's first automobile called the "Quadricycle".
1899	The Boxer Rebellion begins.
1900	Because of the Boxer Rebellion, Americans are forced to evacuate Shantung Province in July 1900, and Lottie takes a job teaching English in Japan and does not return to China until April 1901.
1902	Lottie takes her third furlough to the United States, returning to China in February 1904.
1903	The Wright brothers take their first flights at Kitty Hawk, South Carolina.
1907	R. J. Willingham, head of the Foreign Mission Board of the Southern Baptist Church, visits North China.
1909	Lottie learns of her sister Eddie's death.
1911	The Chinese Revolution begins, attempting to overthrow the dynasty system and make China a republic.
1912	The *RMS Titanic* sinks in the North Atlantic.
1912	Lottie Moon dies on board a ship in Kobe, Japan while traveling to the United States for medical treatment, aged 72 years old.
1918	The Lottie Moon Christmas Offering is officially established.

Thinking Further Topics

Chapter 1: A Training College Trickster
The last part of Numbers 32:23 says "…be sure your sin will find you out." How does this verse apply to Lottie Moon's prankster lifestyle? Have you ever done something wrong that you thought no one knew about? Describe how this verse has been true in your life and how it was true in Lottie's life.

Chapter 2: Facing the Future
Read Psalm 144:15. Can you make a connection between this verse and Lottie's spirits when she came home to Viewmont after her graduation from the Virginia Female Seminary? If people who follow God are happy, do you think those who don't follow God are unhappy? Why or why not?

Chapter 3: Resistance is Futile
The Bible tells us we become new creations when we put our trust in Christ. Compare and contrast Lottie's life before trusting in Jesus with her life after she became a believer. What differences do you see? In what ways did Lottie become a new creation? How have you experienced God's transforming power in your life?

Chapter 4: A World at War

Proverbs 3:5-6 talks about trusting God to direct our paths. Do you think Lottie was trusting God to direct her as the Civil War dragged on? Why or why not? Do you find it easy or difficult to trust God with your whole heart? Why? How has God directed your paths?

Chapter 5: PostWar Practicality

After the Civil War ended, the Moon family faced financial struggles, and Lottie also faced emotional needs as she worked far away from home. Philippians 4:19 says, "But my God shall supply all your needs according to His riches in glory." How did God meet Lottie's needs during these difficult times? How has God provided for the needs in your life?

Chapter 6: The Makings of a Missionary

When God calls us to do something, like He called Lottie to go to China, there are many different ways we can answer. Lottie answered just like the prophet Isaiah, saying, "Here am I, send me" (Isaiah 6:8). Has God called you to do something for Him? How have you answered Him?

Chapter 7: To the Edge of the World and Beyond

Read Isaiah 43:2. How does this verse reflect Lottie's journey to China? Why was she so sure God was with her? Have you ever experienced a difficult or scary time in your life? Were you sure God was with you? How did you know?

Chapter 8: Evangelistic Excursion
Luke 10:2 says, "…the harvest truly is great, but the labourers are few; pray ye therefore the Lord of the harvest, that He would send forth labourers into his harvest." What does the "harvest" represent in that verse? What kind of harvest did Lottie see in China? Do you think only "official" missionaries can help in this harvest? Explain your answer.

Chapter 9: Mrs. Lan's Missionfield
The people in Mrs. Lan's village were eager to hear and understand God's Word. In Matthew 5:6, Jesus said, "Blessed are they which do hunger and thirst after righteousness…" Do you think we often see people hungering and thirsting after righteousness in our modern world? Why or why not?

Chapter 10: Setbacks and Struggles
Read Job 23:10. Lottie Moon definitely faced some tough times during her days as a missionary in China. How do you think these challenges helped her "come forth as gold," as the verse says? How have difficult times in your life helped you become a better person?

Chapter 11: The Challenge of Change
Psalm 118:14 says, "The Lord is my strength and song, and is become my salvation." In what ways do you think Lottie relied on God to be her strength? How did God fuel Lottie's loving spirit? How can God help

you accomplish His will in your life? Give examples to support your answer.

Chapter 12: For the Record

It has been said, "The pen is mightier than the sword." How do you think Lottie used her talent for writing to help accomplish God's purposes? Do you think she was effective? Why or why not? What talents do you have? How could you use those talents for God?

Chapter 13: A New Network

In early 1882, Lottie was excited that new missionaries were arriving in China and her vision was about to become a reality. Just a few years later, she was discouraged by tragedy and thought her vision was over. Read Isaiah 40:31. Did Lottie wait on the Lord? What did He do in response to her trust in Him? In what areas of your life should you be waiting on the Lord a little more? Explain.

Chapter 14: The P'ingtu Project

John 13:35 says, "By this shall all men know that ye are my disciples, if ye have love one to another." How did Lottie show love to the people of P'ingtu? In what ways did this help them accept her? Name some specific ways you can show love to the people around you.

Chapter 15: Sharing in Sha-ling

Read Jeremiah 33:3. What are some of the "great and mighty" things God did in Lottie's ministry? Do you think the establishment of the church at Sha-ling was mostly accomplished by Lottie or by God? Explain your answer. What "great and mighty things" is God doing in your life?

Chapter 16: Fear versus Faith

Members of the Chinese churches often faced persecution and fear. 1 John 4:18 tells us, "...perfect love casteth out fear." What does that mean? Do you think Lottie ever felt fear as she faced scary situations? How do you think she overcame the fear she felt? How can God's love help you overcome fears in your life?

Chapter 17: Christianity in Crisis

Read John 10:10. What does it mean when God says He wants believers to have life "more abundantly?" How do you think this verse might have motivated Lottie's missionary work? What steps could you take to live a more abundant life in Jesus?

Chapter 18: Running from the Rebellion

Lottie loved China and the people who lived there. But during the Boxer Rebellion, she had to serve God somewhere else. Colossians 3:17 says, "And whatsoever ye do in word or deed, do all in the name of the Lord Jesus..." Whatever Lottie did and wherever she went, she served God with all her heart. What can you learn from Lottie's example? How can you serve God in any circumstance?

Chapter 19: The Relief of Return

Although Lottie was growing older, she was still working faithfully. Read Ecclesiastes 9:10. How does this verse relate to Lottie's life? What does it say about laziness? Do you work at things with all your might, just like Lottie did? Explain your answer.

Chapter 20: Battlefield Bravery

Philippians 4:13 says, "I can do all things through Christ, which strengtheneth me." Do you think Lottie thought of this verse much during her ministry in China? What impossibilities—or virtual impossibilities—did God accomplish through His strength in Lottie's life? How has God's strength helped you accomplish great things in your life? Give an example.

Chapter 21: A Lasting Legacy

Read Philippians 1:6. Did God finish His work in Lottie Moon? How did her faithfulness lead to God accomplishing great things in her life? What work do you think God is faithfully completing in your life? What will your personal legacy be?

Author's Notes

When I started this project, I knew little more than Lottie Moon's name. But the more I researched her life, the more I developed a deep love and respect for this tiny, incorrigible, determined lady. Though her energy came in a surprisingly little, 4-foot-3-inch package, her impact was larger than life. She was known for her courage, compassion, honesty, and undying love. I saw in her life so many things I wanted to develop in my own life, and I found myself inspired and motivated.

I read nearly half a dozen biographies on Lottie Moon, scoured prints of some of her personal correspondence, studied pictures of both Lottie and the people she reached, and researched the areas of North China in which she worked. By the end of my information gathering, I felt almost as if I knew Lottie personally. Her life seemed to jump off the page, reaching out across time and miles to encourage me in my own walk and ministry.

So, what made Lottie's life so remarkable and her work so successful? I believe there are four key factors. First, Lottie was willing to do whatever God wanted her to do. Second, Lottie was in tune with God's Spirit and listened carefully to God's direction for her life.

Next, when she knew God's will, she plunged ahead, being as authentic and fearless as she could. Finally, Lottie made sure love was interwoven into every vision, every outreach, and every interaction of her ministry. And ultimately, it was Lottie's love that won the hearts of the Chinese people.

Lottie's legacy is ongoing, more than a century after her death. She transformed mission outreaches and blazed new trails for single female missionaries. She wouldn't listen to those who said she couldn't do things or didn't have the strength, stature, or resources to change her corner of the world. Instead, she listened to the still, small voice of her Heavenly Father and did her best to accomplish His will without compromise. It didn't matter when or where or how, Lottie was determined to persist in making a difference and changing China for Christ. In so many ways, she ideally illustrated Ecclesiastes 9:10: "Whatsoever thy hand findeth to do, do it with thy might …"

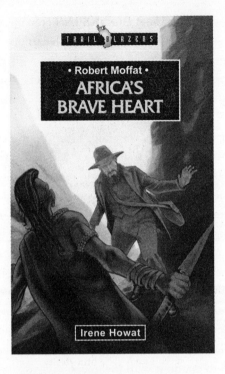

Robert Moffat, Africa's Brave Heart
by Irene Howat
ISBN 978-1-84550-715-2

The story of a Scottish minister and his wife in Africa
– the precursors to David Livingstone. With a sword,
a shovel, a Bible, and great courage, Robert used the
skills he had learned growing up in a Scottish village
to translate the Bible into Tswana and to share God's
love with Africa.

OTHER BOOKS IN THE
TRAILBLAZER SERIES

Augustine, The Truth Seeker
ISBN 978-1-78191-296-6
David Brainerd, A Love for the Lost
ISBN 978-1-84550-695-7
Paul Brand, The Shoes that Love Made
ISBN 978-1-84550-630-8
John Bunyan, The Journey of a Pilgrim
ISBN 978-1-84550-458-8
John Calvin, After Darkness Light
ISBN 978-1-84550-084-9
Fanny Crosby, The Blind Girl's Song
ISBN 978-1-78191-163-1
Billy Graham, Just Get Up Out Of Your Seat
ISBN 978-1-84550-095-5
John Knox, The Sharpened Sword
ISBN 978-1-78191-057-3
C.S. Lewis, The Storyteller
ISBN 978-1-85792-487-9
Eric Liddell, Finish the Race
ISBN 978-1-84550-590-5
Robert Moffat, Africa's Brave Heart
ISBN 978-1-84550-715-2
John Newton, A Slave Set Free
ISBN 978-1-78191-350-5
Mary of Orange, At the Mercy of Kings
ISBN 978-1-84550-818-0
John Stott, The Humble Leader
ISBN 978-1-84550-787-9

CHRISTIAN FOCUS PUBLICATIONS

Christian Focus Christian Heritage CF4K Mentor

Christian Focus Publications publishes books for adults and children under its four main imprints: Christian Focus, CF4K, Mentor and Christian Heritage. Our books reflect our conviction that God's Word is reliable and Jesus is the way to know him, and live for ever with him.

Our children's publication list includes a Sunday School curriculum that covers pre-school to early teens, and puzzle and activity books. We also publish personal and family devotional titles, biographies and inspirational stories that children will love.

If you are looking for quality Bible teaching for children then we have an excellent range of Bible stories and age-specific theological books.

From pre-school board books to teenage apologetics, we have it covered!

Find us at our web page:
www.christianfocus.com

CF4·K
Because you're never
too young to know Jesus